55p
1/4

THE GODS AND THEIR GRAND DESIGN

Also by ERICH VON DÄNIKEN

Chariots of the Gods
Return to the Stars
The Gold of the Gods
Miracles of the Gods
According to the Evidence
Signs of the Gods?
The Stones of Kiribati

THE GODS
AND THEIR
GRAND DESIGN

The Eighth Wonder
of the World

by
ERICH VON DÄNIKEN

Translated by Michael Heron

SOUVENIR PRESS

ISBN 0 285 62630 2

Printed in Great Britain by
Richard Clay (The Chaucer Press) Ltd,
Bungay, Suffolk
Filmset in 'Monophoto' Times by
Northumberland Press Ltd, Gateshead

Contents

1 Legendary Times!   1
2 In the Beginning Everything Was Different   32
3 A Case for Heinrich Schliemann   75
4 The Strategy of the Gods   102
  (As Seen from Colombia)
5 The Eighth Wonder of the World   172
  Picture Acknowledgements   205
  Bibliography   207
  Index   215
  Introduction to the Ancient Astronaut Society   218

1 Legendary Times!

'We should not fear those who hold different opinions, but those who hold different opinions and are too cowardly to say so.'
Napoleon 1 (1769–1821)

Reality is more fantastic than any fantasy.

Before I can follow a trail that was laid many thousands of years ago, I must tell you about an astounding but controversial event that took place in America in the first third of the last century. It leads us back to that ancient trail.

Among the immigrants who streamed into the New World from Germany, Scandinavia, Ireland and England was the Smith family from Scotland, who lived in the small town of Palmyra in New York State.

The district in which the Smiths lived was still barely civilised. Day-to-day existence demanded hard physical toil from the immigrants. The American War of Independence from 1776 to 1783 already lay fifty years behind, but the vast country was still very sparsely inhabited and the settlers had to maintain running battles with the indigenous Indians.

The new arrivals from Europe were hard-working. Not only did they bring tools and goodwill with them, but also the many and varied religions of their homelands, which they sought to propagate with missionary zeal. Sects and religious groups spread like weeds. The apostles of salvation of countless different faiths vied with each other in making extravagant promises and capturing souls with sinister threats about the hereafter. Chapels, temples and churches shot up like mushrooms, as though the devil himself had discovered how to confuse the minds of the settlers in their new homeland.

Like many immigrants, Mother Smith and her three children were Presbyterians. Her son Joseph, who was eighteen, found things more difficult. He sought desperately for the true God, because he could not accept the fact that all the saviours claimed firmly to be in the right and at the same time fought each other bitterly in the name of Jesus. Joseph Smith (1805–1844) was a nonentity, until the night of 21 September 1823, when he had a strange vision.

Joseph was praying fervently in his bedroom, when he suddenly perceived a light, which illuminated the room brilliantly. A bare-footed angel in a white robe stepped out of the light. The vision introduced himself to the terrified youth as Moroni, the messenger of God. Moroni had astounding news for the young man!

The angel told him that in a stony hiding-place near the Smith family's home town a book was preserved written on gold plates and giving a full account of the former inhabitants

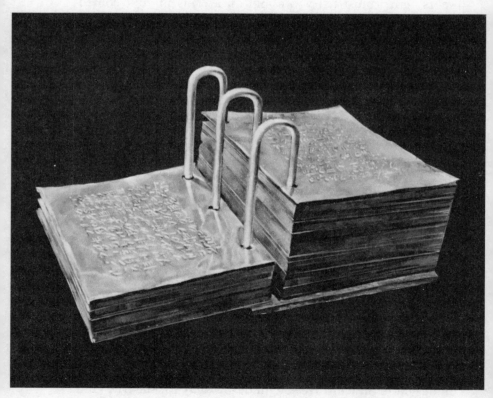

The Book of Mormon, inscribed on gold plates, revealed to Joseph Smith through a vision.

of the American continent and the source from whence they came. Near the gold tablets lay a breastplate to which two stones, Urim and Thummim,* were attached and with their help the ancient scripture could be translated. In addition the cache contained a divine compass. After telling Joseph Smith that he had been chosen to translate part of the scriptures and spread their message abroad, Moroni, the divine messenger, vanished.

Only for a while.

Then he reappeared, repeated the exciting news and added the prophecy that there would be great desolation by famine, sword and pestilence in the future.

We do not know whether Moroni was ordered to deliver his message bit by bit or whether he was forgetful. In any case he appeared for the third time on the night of 21 September to add a warning to his two previous messages. Joseph was forbidden to show the sacred objects on the Hill of Cumorah to anyone, apart from a chosen few. If he broke this commandment he would be killed.

Short of sleep after his nocturnal visit, Joseph naturally told his father about his alarming experience over their frugal breakfast. A bigoted believer like all the settlers, Father Smith had no doubt that his son had been given a divine mission — to seek out the place described by the angel Moroni.

South of Palmyra, near the village of Manchester, rises the Hill of Cumorah, which towers up steeply on its north side. Underneath the top of the hill Joseph Smith found the treasure he had been promised. This is how he himself described it:

Under a stone of considerable size lay the plates, deposited in a stone box. This stone was thicker and rounding in the middle on the upper side and thinner towards the edges, so that the middle part of it was visible above the ground, but the edge round was covered with earth. Having removed the earth, I obtained a lever, which I got fixed under the edge of the stone, and with a little exertion raised it up. I looked in, and there indeed did I behold the plates. The box in which they lay was formed by laying stones together in some kind of cement. In the bottom of the box were laid two stones

* Oracle stones used by the priests of Israel.

The Hill of Cumorah beneath whose summit Joseph Smith found the buried treasure, the plates of the Book of Mormon.

crossways of the box, and on these stones lay the plates and the other things with them.

When the teenager, with the curiosity of any treasure-hunter, automatically reached for the objects with both hands, he immediately felt a blow. He tried again and received another crippling blow. At the third attempt he received what seemed like a powerful electric shock. He lay on the floor as if paralysed.

At the same moment Moroni, the enigmatic nocturnal messenger, appeared beside him and ordered Joseph to return there every year on the same day. When the time was ripe, he would be given the sacred objects.

That time came four years later.

On 22 September 1827 the heavenly messenger Moroni handed Joseph Smith the engraved gold plates, the breastplate and the gleaming translation aids Urim and Thummim. Moroni impressed on the 22-year-old Joseph that he would be held responsible if the ancient treasures were lost owing to his carelessness.

I do not know if this story really took place like that. However that is exactly how it is handed down in *The Book of Mormon*, the 'Bible' of 'The Church of Jesus Christ of Latter-day Saints', the Mormons. It is the firm belief of several million Mormons, those devout people who have their headquarters in Salt Lake City in the State of Utah.

I do not know whether Joseph Smith was a religious psychopath or a crafty demagogue who took advantage of the religious confusion of his day to ensnare people. I do not know if Joseph Smith was a selfless, honourable truth-seeking prophet.

Nor do I know who visited the young man on the night of 21 September 1823 and handed over the hidden treasure four years later. Was it an Indian who knew of the existence of the ancient plates? Could he, or a member of his tribe, have hidden them? Did an Indian convert to one of the many Christian communities betray a well-preserved secret? Did a white treasure-hunter, who needed a partner, initiate Joseph Smith? Or did the young man stumble on the treasure trove alone and invent the story of the heavenly vision to attract attention?

I do not know the answer, but one thing seems certain. Joseph Smith actually possessed the engraved gold plates!

With the help of the 'translation stones' Urim and Thummim, Joseph Smith had worked for 21 months translating part of the text on the plates before he showed them to three honourable and respected men in June 1829 — with the angel Moroni's permission, of course! Oliver Cowdery, David Whitmer and Martin Harris drew up a document in which they swore that they had seen the plates 'and the engravings thereon'.

This testimony carries some weight, for the three men stuck to it after they had parted from Smith and the Church of Latter-day Saints he founded, two of them even becoming violent opponents of the new religion. None of the men disavowed his oath.

Two days after revealing the engraved plates to the three men, Smith showed his treasure to eight more witnesses, who were allowed to handle the thin plates and leaf through them. These eight men also testified to the fact with their seals and signatures (2):

> Be it known to all nations, kindreds, tongues and people, unto whom this work shall come: That Joseph Smith, Jun., the translator of this work, has shown unto us the plates of which hath been spoken, which have the appearance of gold; and as many of the leaves as the said Smith has translated we did handle with our hands; and we also saw the engravings thereon, all of which have the appearance of ancient work, and of curious workmanship. And this we bear record with words of soberness, that the said Smith has shown unto us, for we have seen and hefted, and know of a surety that the said Smith has got the plates of which we have spoken. And we give our names unto the world, to witness unto the world that which we have seen. And we lie not, God bearing witness of it.
> CHRISTIAN WHITMER. JACOB WHITMER. PETER WHITMER JUN. JOHN WHITMER. HIRAM PAGE. JOSEPH SMITH SEN. HYRUM SMITH. SAMUEL H. SMITH.

The oaths of 11 men, not all members of the religious community founded by Joseph Smith, who defended their

Characters which Joseph Smith copied from the metal plates. Scholars classified them as 'reformed Egyptian hieroglyphs'.

ancient faith belligerently and called on their God as witness, carry considerable weight, if we remember the fantastic zeal with which the settlers clung to their congregations and sects for fear of punishment at the Last Judgement.

The two sworn testimonies are not alone in supporting the conclusion that Smith actually possessed the engraved plates for a time, the contents of the translation also support it. They exclude a *complete* forgery, although I am sure there was *partial* forgery.

Smith described the book's golden plates as somewhat thinner than the tin plate commonly used at the time. The individual pages were held together by three rings. The book was some 15 cm broad, 20 cm high and 15 cm thick. A third of the metal pages could be leafed through easily, the other two-thirds being 'sealed' to a block. Smith made copies of the characters on the plates and these were later classified by scholars as 'reformed Egyptian hieroglyphs'.

The present-day Book of Mormon of the Church of Jesus Christ of Latter-day Saints, based on the translations of the mysterious plates by the church's founder Joseph Smith, enlarged by the addition of prophecies about Jesus (which were certainly not in the original text) and a kind of continuation of biblical history, fitted in well with the Christian faith of American society around the middle of the last century.

Smith and his Church of Jesus Christ of Latter-day Saints soon became the object of mockery, but they also attracted the hostility of the American fundamentalists, who stuck rigorously to a literal interpretation of the Bible and preached zealously against critical theology and modern science. There are still fundamentalists in America today.

It was a painful business for Smith because, after their successful translation, the angel Moroni asked for the plates back to hide them again for the distant future. So apart from this translation and the sworn statements of the 11 men, poor Joseph had no proof that he had actually held the legendary plates in his hands every day for nearly two years.

The young Mormon community fought bravely and kept its spirits up. In spite of constant persecution, it increased in size and has 5 million adherents today, although internal strife in the early days led to the arrest of Joseph and his brother Hyrum. On 27 June 1844 a mob broke into the jail at Carthago, Illinois, and shot the brothers Smith. The industrious and God-fearing Mormons had their martyrs. They stuck together and during the last 140 years created a religious and secular empire without parallel.

Between past millennia and the last century there is only a rickety suspension-bridge over a perilous abyss and that is loosely anchored to the banks of time. In spite of that, many rotten planks force researchers to make reckless leaps unless they want to sink in the morass of the present. Two sections of the Book of Mormon, the plates of Ether and Nephi, are well suited to form a fairly solid bridge leading back to past millennia.

The 24 plates of Ether tell the story of the people of Jared. According to the translated plates, the Jaredites are supposed to have pleaded with their God about the time of the building of the Tower of Babel, i.e. towards the end of 3,000 BC, to save them from the warlike turmoil of the neighbouring peoples. God heard their plea and led the Jaredites in a spectacular trek, first into a wilderness and then across the ocean to the coast of America. The journey, described in great detail, lasted 344 days. The plates do not state on which coast of the American continent the emigrants landed, but extracts from the Mormon Bible, Book of Ether, 2. 4 *et seq.*, may be of interest:

And it came to pass that when they came down into the valley of Nimrod [Mesopotamia, E.v.D.] the Lord came down and talked with the brother of Jared; and he was in a cloud and the brother of Jared saw him not.

And it came to pass that the Lord did go before them and did talk with them as he stood in a cloud, and gave directions whither they should travel. And it came to pass that they did travel in the wilderness, and did build barges, in which they did cross many waters, being directed continually by the hand of the Lord.

The barges were small and light upon the water, even like unto the likeness of a fowl upon the water.

And they were built after a manner that they were exceedingly tight, even that they would hold water like unto a dish; and the ends thereof were peaked; and the top thereof was tight and like unto a dish; and the length thereof was the length of a tree; and the door thereof, when it was shut, was tight like unto a dish.

When the Jaredites had built eight windowless watertight vessels according to their 'Lord's' instructions, they thought they noticed a structural error. When the only door was closed, it was pitch black on board, but obviously it was not a mistake, for the 'Lord' gave them 16 gleaming stones, two for each vessel, and the stones gave them bright light for 344 days. Great stuff!

The craft, loaded with seeds and small animals of all kinds, must have been amazingly manoeuvrable in all weathers. Even if the translation of the Book of Ether is only partly factual, the technology the 'Lord' passed on to the Jaredites was sensational. This quotation makes amazing reading:

And it came to pass that they were many times buried in the depths of the sea, because of the mountain waves which broke upon them, and also the great and terrible tempests which were caused by the fierceness of the wind.

And it came to pass that when they were buried in the deep there was no water that could hurt them, their vessel being tight like unto a dish, and also they were tight like unto the ark of Noah; therefore when they were encompassed about by many waters they did cry unto the Lord, and he did bring them forth again upon the top of the waters.

First God created man, then he destroyed his descendants in the Flood. He made a covenant with the survivors 'for all future generations' (Genesis 9.10 *et seq.*). Rebellious mankind tried to rival God and built the mighty tower of Babel. God descended in a rage and scattered the children of men 'over the face of all the earth' (Genesis 11.1 *et seq.*). One of these exiled groups was the Jaredites, who were transported to America in vessels light as birds, with strange sources of light.

If God wanted to give a group of people a chance of survival, what was the point of the laborious construction of eight small vessels? Could not almighty God have carried them to distant parts by a miracle?

Couldn't this God have flown the Jaredites over the ocean or did he prefer not to? Their presence in America shows that he wanted to help them cross the big pond. Was he only able to give technical instructions for ship-building? If he forgot that it was pitch-dark inside the ships, was he forced to correct his error in retrospect by providing flashing stones? Even if the Lord did not want to perform a miracle, even if he made these people work hard for their salvation, why did he not give instructions for building a normal surface craft which could have crossed the Atlantic comfortably? And if the craft had to be like nutshells, almighty God, the acknowledged Lord of the clouds and winds, could at least have given his flock calm seas.

It annoys me that an everlasting omniscient God could not see any farther into the future. Did he not sense that thousands of years after the ocean crossing the traditional account might provoke doubts about his omnipotence? Did it spark the question why technology and not a miracle? He would have been wiser to make use of a miracle which would be inexplicable for all eternity. Miracles escape the bounds of critical reason.

Like all immigrants, the Jaredites sailed to America in terrible conditions. Did not their guardian 'Lord' possess adequate technology to transport his protégés over the big pond in a less dangerous way? What kind of 'God' was at work here 5,000 years ago?

The literature of dark distant ages is literally legendary. We have no precise knowledge. Mankind, stupid and incorrigible, has always managed to wipe out the traditions of previous ages. The library of the ancient city of Pergamon in Asia

Minor, with its 500,000 volumes, was destroyed. The great libraries of ancient Jerusalem and Alexandria were destroyed; the libraries of the Aztecs and Maya went up in flames. Successive generations of mankind wiped out the collected wisdom of the past, but they did not wipe it out completely. There still exist fragments of age-old traditions from which, with a little ingenuity, we can form conceptions of the 'gods' who were once active. We cannot now determine the age of the traditions from textual fragments. The chroniclers noted down indiscriminately not only what they experienced, but also what they knew only from hearsay. Primeval, old and 'new' stories were woven into a colourful tapestry. The chonological course of events was mixed as if in a cocktail-shaker. The years drew rings, but over the centuries collected around a central point.

All we have to do today is to peel off the layers of this 'onion' in order to reveal the essential core. Getting at the 'hard core' is not really miraculous or inexplicable. It is a matter for reason, i.e. analysis, and hence explicable. Working outwards from the centre of tradition — freed of chance superficial accretions — we can find trails which were once expounded for curious men in the distant future. This future has actually begun!

The *Sagen der Juden von der Urzeit* (3) (Legends of the Jews from Primitive Times) relate that, after the banishment from Paradise, the angel Raziel gave Adam a book 'at the behest of the All Highest', the text of which was clearly engraved 'on a sapphire stone'.

Raziel told Adam that he could educate himself with the help of this book. Our first ancestor realised how valuable the 'book' was and after reading it he always hid it in a cave.

Adam learnt from the engravings:

everything about his limbs and veins and all things that went on inside his body and their purpose and causes. He also learnt about the courses of the planets. With the aid of the book he could ... examine the paths of the moon and the paths of Aldebaran, Orion and Sirius. He could name the names of every separate heaven and knew wherein the activity of each one consisted ... Adam knew all about the rolling thunder, he could tell the action of lightning and could narrate what would happen from moon to moon.

A 'book' on a sapphire stone giving anthropological and astronomical instruction? The heavenly messenger Raziel's gift to Adam is as grotesque as the one Moroni gave to Joseph Smith!

For chroniclers in the remote past all this must have been rather like what journalists today call a canard, a phoney story. This 'book' on a sapphire stone was sheer nonsense.

As clever children of the computer age, we know that things that were once inconceivable are technically possible now. Everyone knows that technology uses tiny silicon chips on which to 'engrave', i.e. store, millions of bits of information. Looking at it from a modern point of view we may ask ourselves if the transmission of a text on a sapphire stone was the product of an advanced technology already far ahead of our own.

The *Sagen der Juden von der Urzeit* has it that Adam handed the book down to his son Seth and that it was inherited by his descendants Enoch, Noah, Abraham, Moses, Aaron and then by Solomon (c. 965–926 BC), the King of Judah and Israel, who acquired his enormous wisdom from the sapphire stone.

According to the *Sagen der Juden von Urzeit*, the Book of the Prophet Enoch was supposed to have formed part of Adam's sapphire book. Enoch, the seventh of the ten patriarchs, was in direct touch with God and spoke to the 'Watchers of the Heavens' and the 'fallen angels'. At the age of 365 he was carried up to heaven — without dying — in a spectacular fashion. Ancient Jewish legends go on to say that Enoch acquired his all-embracing knowledge from Adam's book and that men gathered round him so that he could spread the wisdom of the sapphire stone, teach and instruct them:

When the men sat around Enoch and Enoch spoke to them, they raised their eyes and saw the form of a steed come down from heaven, and the steed descended to earth in a storm. Then the people told Enoch and Enoch spoke unto them: This steed has descended for my sake. The time has come and the day when I go from you and from which day forth I shall never see you again. Then the steed was there and stood before Enoch and all the children of men saw it clearly.

Ancient Jewish tradition describes how the faithful did not

want to let Enoch go after his eloquent farewell before his ascent into heaven, how they ran after him and how he bade them seven times to leave him alone, how he insistently warned them to turn round, for otherwise they would die. It says that small groups of people went home after each warning, although the most persistent stayed with Enoch. Loyalty, devotion, curiosity? In the end Enoch gave up; he lost his temper!

As they insisted on going with him, he spoke to them no longer, and they followed him and did not turn back. And on the seventh day it came to pass that Enoch rode up to heaven in a storm on fiery steeds in fiery chariots.

The ancient Jewish legend shows that events at Enoch's take-off for heaven unfolded in the most 'ungodly' way. When things had quietened down, those who had heeded Enoch's warning and returned home went looking for their friends who had stuck to the prophet until the countdown. They all lay dead around the launching-pad — excuse me — the spot from which Enoch ascended with the fiery steeds.

The legendary age between Adam's appearance in the scenario of the history of mankind and the building of the tower of Babel was the first great age of the gods, of fire-breathing horses, mysterious deaths and remarkable births.

The story, then, is as old as the hills, although we have only known about it since 1947. That was when sensational finds were made in eleven mountain caves at the north-west end of the Dead Sea, near Qumran. They consisted of numerous manuscripts from the second century BC written on leather scrolls concealed in earthenware jars.

One scroll tells the story of Lamech, Noah's father and patron of nomads and musicians.

Even on the Other Side, Lamech will be glad that his intimate family history was not generally known during his lifetime, it was so painful and remarkable. Lamech's wife Bat Enosh gave birth to a child, although the head of the family had never slept with her. Later Lamech learnt from his grand-father Enoch that the 'Watchers of the Heavens' had placed the seeds in Bat Enosh's womb. Lamech showed great generosity and recognised the child as his own. The offspring produced in this remarkable way was called Noah at the request of the 'Watchers'. The same Noah became world famous as a survivor of the Flood.

To make matters worse, the arrival of an unnaturally begotten child in the family of Lamech's son Nir could not be concealed. Nir was married to Sopranima and she was barren, to the family's sorrow. Nir tried hard to implant progeny in Sopranima's womb, but without success. For a priest of the Almighty like Nir, admired by the common people for his wisdom, it was a terrible scandal to learn that Sopranima was barren. Nir was shattered and reviled his wife so grossly that she collapsed and died, although a boy the size of a three-year-old crawled out of his mother's womb. Nir summoned Noah. They buried Sopranima and called the little boy Melchizedek, thenceforth known as the legendary priest-king of Salem, later Jerusalem (5).

Tradition leaves us in no doubt that Melchizedek was a case of a 'divine birth'. Before the Lord opened the sluices to unleash the Flood, the Archangel Michael came down from heaven and informed adoptive father Nir that it was the 'Lord' who had implanted the boy in Sopranima's womb. Consequently, and we can understand this, the Lord had sent him, Archangel Michael, with orders to carry the boy Melchizedek to Paradise so that he would survive the imminent deluge safely:

> And Michael took the boy on the very night on which he had descended and took him on his wings and set him in the Paradise of Eden.

Melchizedek survived! He reappears after the Flood. Moses tells us about it:

> After his return from the defeat of Ched-or-laomer and the kings who were with him, the king of Sodom went out to meet him at the Valley of Shaveh (that is, the Kings' Valley). And Melchizedek king of Salem brought out bread and wine; he was priest of God Most High. And he blessed him and said, 'Blessed be Abram by God Most High, maker of heaven and earth, and blessed be God Most High, who has

delivered your enemies into your hands!' And Abram gave him a tenth of everything.

(Genesis 14.17–20)

Hundreds of Old Testament scholars and exegetists have been excited by this passage from the Bible. 'The strange figure of the priest — king of Salem, who appears like a *deux ex machina* and then vanishes again — has naturally interested posterity' (8).

Obviously, because something extraordinary happened here. Abraham, the first of the three Patriarchs, stands at the head of Jewish tradition. Then the almost unknown Melchizedek comes along and blesses him! And that is not all. Of his own accord, the patriarch gives the king of Salem 'a tenth of everything!' What kind of a priest of 'God Most High' was that? After all, there was only the one God, whom Abraham worshipped. Or did Abraham know anything about the most extraordinary 'divine' birth? Melchizedek appears unexpectedly; he cannot be fitted into any tailor-made accepted pattern.

Given a little less naive faith and a little more courage, the Melchizedek mystery could be solved by modern speculation in this way. An extraterrestrial crew made up of so-called gods produced Noah and Melchizedek by artificial insemination. The legal fathers, Lamech and Noah, recognise them as their own sons, but against their better judgement, for they remember the assurances that the sons of the heavenly ones would be responsible for the artificial insemination of their wives Bat Enosh and Sopranima. It was the same heavenly gods who destroyed their descendants because their genetic experiment did not develop as they liked. Saved from the Flood, both were the products of genetic manipulation. As captain of the ark Noah became founder of the new generation and the priest king Melchizedek became its teacher.

The fact that Melchizedek existed both before and after the Flood does not conflict with this theory. What Albert Einstein calculated with his special theory of relativity and what was proved in physical experiments makes it possible. If Melchizedek, thanks to Archangel Michael's friendly cooperation, boarded a spaceship that accelerated to very high speeds and came straight back to earth, decades or centuries would have passed on earth, whereas the crew of the spaceship would not have aged significantly before they landed again. Melchizedek would still be young and eager for new tasks.*

It is not a question of names or the lapse of time. 'Legendary' traditions cannot be arranged chronologically. Was the survivor of the Flood really called Noah, as the Bible claims? Or was his name Utnapishtim, as it says in the Sumerian *Epic of Gilgamesh*, which dates from c. 2,000 BC? Or was the survivor of the Flood not even called Utnapishtim, but Mulkueikai, as the Kágaba Indians of Colombia name the priest who survived the Flood in a magic craft? Names are unimportant. What matters is the substance of the traditions.

Have we lost sight of Joseph Smith's Book of Mormon? What have the angel Raziel, Enoch's ascent into heaven and the artificial procreation of Noah and Melchizedek got to do with the Book of Mormon?

In the Book of Ether translated by Smith it says that the Jaredites were sent to sea in their eight ships around the time of the building of the Tower of Babel. The Jaredites were led by one of Jared's brothers and Jared himself was Enoch's father!

Jared means something like 'He who has come down', so it is understandable that the Jaredites were a race from a 'divine line' and so enjoyed the privilege of being introduced to a new country by the gods after the Flood. The crew of the spaceship looked after their descendants. They seem to me to have invented the nepotism so widely practised today.

To recapitulate, in the Book of Ether the Jaredites come to their new home in eight windowless ships, each one as tight as a dish. A similar crossing is described in the Babylonian didactic poem about the creation, the *Enuma elis*. It, too, gives an account of the Flood, but this time the survivor is called Atrahasis (9). In the partially preserved epic the god Enki gives the man chosen for survival, Atrahasis, precise instructions for building the ship. In answer to Atrahasis' objection that he knows nothing about ship-building, Enki draws the outline of a ship on the ground and enlightens him.

The American orientalist Zecharia Sitchin, the first scholar bold enough to interpret Sumerian, Assyrian, Babylonian and biblical texts in a modern way, writes (10) that Enki demanded a well-planned ship, hermetically sealed all round and caulked

* See my book *According to the Evidence* (1977) for other biblical characters exposed to the effects of time dilation.

with strong pitch. There were to be no deck or openings so that sun could not shine in. It was to be like an *aspu* ship, a *sulili*, (the same word (soleleth) that is used in Hebrew today for a submarine). Enki asked for the ship to be a MA-GUr-Gur (a ship that can roll and be tossed about).

Joseph Smith held the gold plates in his hands in 1827. The poor immigrant from Scotland knew neither Aramaic nor ancient Hebrew and he had never seen Sumerian cuneiform writing. Indeed, in the days of the Mormon prophet there was no scholar in the world who could have deciphered the Babylonian tablets, because, like the Epic of Gilgamesh, they were not discovered until after Joseph Smith's death. So how can we explain the similarities between the Book of Ether and the other texts discovered later?

Our contemporaries see history through glasses polished by scholars. In so far as glasses from the workshops of the exact sciences — mathematics, physics, biology and chemistry, for example, — are concerned, they improve the sight. But since theology and psychology have been given the status of sciences, the glasses have become blurred. Those two disciplines should have been left to the blissful field of faith. When theologists and psychologists agitate old texts in the cocktail-shaker of their specialties, only turbid faith trickles out. And we are supposed to swallow that as if it were a scientific conclusion!

Although expressed more elegantly in the circumlocutions of scientific parlance, it is clearly insinuated that the old chroniclers lied. Driven into a corner, they would be more willing to agree (which archaeologists, ethnologists and pre-historians do not) that men were already capable of building seaworthy ships thousands of years ago than that they involved 'gods', alien teachers, in their logical calculations.

Did the chroniclers of the *Enuma elis* epic lie when they wrote that Atrahasis was instructed in ship-building by the god Enki? Why had Noah and Utnapishtim to be given the idea of building watertight and weatherproof ships by gods? In what magic workshop was the artificial lighting for the Jaredites' fleet cooked up? If there were no savants, how can we understand the 'miracle' of artificial fertilisation that nevertheless brought two splendid types like Noah and Melchizedek into the world?

I know that Noah is not a unique case! The oldest Sumerian

Noah was not even Utnapishtim, but the still older Ziusudra. This example clearly shows that various chroniclers obviously (a) drew on earlier sources and (b) gave former heroes the names of their own people. No matter under what names the conquerors of the Flood appear in the ancient traditions, they were all of semi-divine origin. The protagonists were certainly not purely terrestrial!

Anyone who studies the fragmentarily preserved old texts with clear undimmed glasses finds special characteristics to identify the 'gods' by.

Unlike the God dominating the universe, the divine figures of legend and myth were by no means omnipotent. They did not appear like fairies who moved groups of people from one place to another with a wave of their magic wand. To be sure, the 'gods' themselves flew across countries and even took passengers with them in certain cases, but they did not transport groups of men in their varied types of vehicle. This clearly implies that the 'gods' did not use giant spaceships, their technical capabilities being far too limited. We can assume that their craft were more probably a mixture of shuttle and helicopter. The NASA engineer Josef Blumrich has conclusively proved from the Book of Ezekiel that a mini-spaceship could have been constructed in biblical times (11).

A large mother ship in the earth's orbit that men from the Blue Planet never saw launched smaller craft in the direction of the earth. As in the American space shuttle, there was only room for a small crew. Outside the earth's atmosphere the mini-spaceship fell slowly, braked by its ram jet drive, into the thicker atmospheric layers of the earth. The ram jet drive got its energy from a nuclear reactor. (Opponents of atomic energy will complain that the crew would have been contaminated by radioactivity. Nonsense. Why are sailors not contaminated after long voyages in nuclear-powered submarines?)

The mini-spaceship stopped some 10 km above the earth. Then two or three helicopter units firmly attached to the mini-spaceship emerged. (Helicopters with rotor blades cannot emerge, scoff the sceptics. They can, because they are built to fit inside each other, like a car radio aerial. But what about energy? The main reactor supplied that.) The shuttle glided to earth by means of the helicopters and was in a position to land on plains or mountainous terrain. Fantasy? Where did the

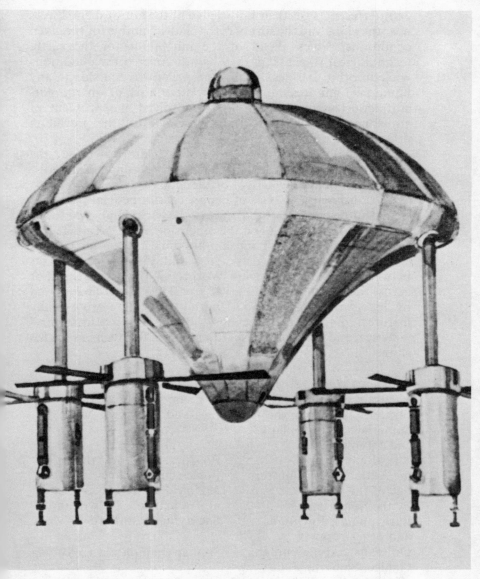

The small spaceship which the NASA engineer Josef F. Blumrich constructed from the details given in the Book of Ezekiel.

extraterrestrials get their knowledge of the atmospheric layers near the globe and the sort of rotor blades suitable for the given conditions? Miles ahead of the inhabitants of the earth, technologically speaking, they had discovered the conditions while in orbit. Besides, a ship's propeller drives a ship in any liquid medium, fresh or salt water, oil or a sea of whisky. Aircraft constructors have long since solved the problem of adjusting rotor blades to the right angle for the prevailing atmospheric pressure.

Incidentally, helicopter landings explain the noise, the thunder and uproar which all the ancient chroniclers describe as accompanying the arrival of the 'gods'.

Obviously large masses of people cannot be transported in small shuttle craft. If a 'god', one of the Most High, wanted to settle a group of peoples on the other side of the ocean, he had to impart instructions about ship-building, as tradition tells us.

Today most ethnologists agree that there were contacts between the Old and the New Worlds, via the Bering Strait or across the Atlantic on simple rafts, as Thor Heyerdahl proved by his own voyages (12). Undoubtedly there were many features common to the civilisations of South and Central America, and those of the Near East, as the following examples show:

Near and Middle East	*South and Central America*
Accurate calendar calculations among the Sumerians, Babylonians and Egyptians	The same is true of the Inca and (later) the Maya
The ability to cut megalithic stone monsters out of the rock. Practised by the Sumerians, Babylonians, Egyptians and other peoples	Pre-Inca tribes and the Inca possessed the same technical ability. Examples at Tiahuanaco, Bolivia and Sacsayhuaman, Peru
Dolmans and menhirs in Galilee, Samaria, Judea (13) also in prehistoric England and France	Similar examples in Colombia
Mummification	Also found
Prehistoric astronomically	The same finds in

Near and Middle East	*South and Central America*
aligned stone circles and rectangles	prehistoric Peru and Colombia
Enormous markings on the ground that point to the sky in the deserts of present-day Saudi Arabia	The same phenomenon in Peru (Nazca, Palpa) and on the coastal cliffs of Chile
Marriage between brothers and sisters among the Babylonians and Egyptian Pharaohs	Incest also among the Inca to preserve the 'divine blood' of the Sun God
Stories of the Flood, including details such as the dove and the raven which signalled the survivors to leave the ark, among the Sumerians, Babylonian and Egyptians	The same tradition among the Kágaba Indians of Colombia and (later) the Aztecs of Mexico The Aztec Noah was called Tapi The Aztec Flood epic is identical with the biblical one
Skull deformation of small children among the Egyptians	The same deliberate deformation among pre-Inca and Inca tribes
Depictions of cranial surgery on living patients among the Babylonians and Egyptians	The same trepannings among the Inca and Central and North American Indians
Great engineering skill in the building of extensive irrigation systems among the Babylonians	The same skill shown by the Inca and Maya. Recently vast canal systems built by the Maya have been mapped from aircraft and satellites (14)
Feather headdresses or crowns were worn to show that people had an affinity with 'that which flies'. Shown to have been used by Egyptian and Hittite popular leaders	The same custom among the Inca and all Indian tribes
Adoration of the 'flying	Inca and Maya edifices

Near and Middle East
snake' among the
Babylonians, Egyptians,
Hittites and other
Mesopotamian peoples
Building pyramids to
honour the gods and get
closer to them

South and Central America
teem with 'flying snakes'

The steeply rising step
pyramids of the Maya do
not resemble the less steep
unstepped pyramids near
Cairo, but there were step
pyramids in Egypt, too,
e.g. at Sakkara. The
massive pyramid of
Teotihuacan, Mexico, is
comparable to the
Egyptian pyramids. The
Mesopotamian ziggurats
are stepped forerunners of
the pyramids

In Genesis 11.1 it says:
'Now the whole earth had
one language and few
words ...'

In the Popol Vuh, (15) the
Quiché Maya creation
myth, in the chapter on
'Completion of Creation'
we read: 'they had a single
language. They prayed to
neither wood nor stone ...'
and in the chapter
'Wanderers through the
Night': 'Lost are we.
Whence the confusion? We
had one language when we
came to Tula.'

In Exodus 14.16 the Lord
says to Moses: 'Lift up
your rod and stretch out
your hand over the sea and
divide it, that the people of
Israel may go on dry
ground through the sea.'

In the traditions of the
Cakchiqueles, a branch of
the Maya, we read: 'Let us
plunge the tips of our rods
into the sand under the sea
and we shall rapidly
control the sea above the
sand. Our red rods, which
we received before the

Near and Middle East

South and Central America
gates of Tula, will aid us
... When we came to the
edge of the sea, Balam
Quitze touched it with his
rod and straightway a way
was opened.'

Exodus 14.21: 'Then Moses
stretched out his hand over
the sea; and the Lord
drove the sea back by a
strong east wind all night,
and made the sea dry land,
and the waters were
divided. And the people of
Israel went into the midst
of the sea on dry ground,
the waters being a wall to
them on their right hand
and their left.'

Popol Vuh, chapter
entitled 'Wanderers
through the Night': 'They
scarcely noticed how they
crossed the sea. They
crossed it as if there were
no sea. Round stones rose
from the sand and over the
rows of stones did they
walk into it. They called
the place drifting sand;
those who crossed the
parting sea have the name.
Thus did they manage to
cross.'

Genesis 9.12: 'This is the
sign of the covenant which
I make between me and
you and every living
creature that is with
you ...'

Popol Vuh, chapter
'Departure of the
Patriarch': 'This will
succour you when you call
on me. This is the sign of
the covenant. But, now,
heavy of heart, I have to
go.'

Daniel 3.21: 'Then these
men were bound in their
mantles, their tunics, their
hats and other garments
and they were cast into the
burning fiery furnace ...
(25) He answered, "But I
see four men loose,
walking in the midst of the
fire, and they are not hurt;
and the appearance of the

Popol Vuh, chapter 'Ball
Game and Kingdom of the
Dead': 'Then those men
went into the fire, into a
fire house. Within all was
burning heat, but they did
not burn. Smooth of body
and fair of face did they
appear in the twilight.
People wished them dead
in the places where they

Near and Middle East	*South and Central America*
fourth is like a son of the gods." '	walked, but it did not happen. Confusion seized those of Xibalba.'

It would be useful to expand the small list of the staggering concordances between ancient texts of the Old and New Worlds in a dissertation the size of a large volume, if there were any real interest in explaining unsolved mysteries of the past.

Thor Heyerdahl drew attention to still more parallels, such as identical techniques for weaving cotton, the similarity in the circumcision of boys, the same gold filigree work and so on (12). The scientific journalist Gerd von Hassler confirmed astonishingly similar names given to gods and cities on both continents (16).

The Popol Vuh removes the last doubt about the importation of civilisation into South and Central America from the Mesopotamian region. It states clearly that the Patriarchs came from the East:

Thus did they vanish and go thither, Balám Quitzé, Balam Acab, Mahucutáh and Jqu Balám, *the first men who came over the sea from the beginning of the sun.* They came hither a long time ago. They died at a great age. And they were called 'Servants of God', Sacrificers' ... *and they brought the writings of Tula over the sea.* They called the scripture that wherein their history was written.

In 1519, when the Spanish conquerors were camped outside Tenochtitlan, Mexico, the Aztec ruler Moctezuma (1466–1520) made an impressive speech to the priests and important dignitaries. It began as follows: 'You know, as I do, *That our forefathers did not come from this country* in which we live, but that they came here *from far, far away* under the guidance of a great prince.'

Moctezuma was a highly cultured ruler of his people, well versed in the sciences of his day, and he had a thorough knowledge of the traditions of his ancestors. He knew what he was talking about. He saw the arrival of the Spaniards under Hernando Cortez as the fulfilment of his belief in the return of the god Quetzalcoatl and so he offered no resistance.

The question no longer arises *whether* civilisations were effectively influenced. What matters is to try to answer the question *when* and *why* they were influenced.

It is pointless to puzzle about the WHEN. In spite of the existence of artefacts which can be dated archaeologically, there is not even an approximate chronology. The Aztecs already referred to ancient traditions, the origins of which they knew nothing. The same was true of the Maya and the Inca. The chroniclers of the day had not experienced what they wrote about: 'It is written in the records of the fathers.' Without quoting sources, I should warn the reader. The authors did not know who these fathers were or when they immigrated.

However, archaeological datings go steadily further back into the past. In *Scientific American*, (18) the celebrated American Maya scholar Norman Hammond mentioned finds of pottery from Yucatán, the northern peninsula between the Gulf of Mexico and the Caribbean, dating to 2,600 years BC. Some of the pre-classical Maya periods may be calculated from the artistic motifs represented on the pottery. The new date confuses us considerably; for according to the previous view held by archaeologists the ancient Maya kingdom was supposed to have begun c. 600 BC and the pre-classical Maya period c. 900 BC at the earliest. So what are we to make of these troublesome potsherds, which are a good 1500 years too old to fit into their theory? Scholars would dearly love to reinter them and forget all about them, leaving a tough nut for future generations to crack. Each new dating complicates the puzzle and yet we anticipate many new finds. The latest academic conclusion is that there is nothing definite about when the legendary immigration took place from either written or archaeological evidence. Dates are still shrouded in the mists of the history of mankind.

HOW the great journey took place is equally obscure. The Bering Strait, icebound in spring and winter, which lies between Cape Prince, Alaska, and Cape Desnef, Siberia, suggests itself as a route. Even today navigation is difficult at all times of the year, owing to drift-ice and fog. This dangerous sea route sounds impracticable for peoples migrating thousands of years ago. But if we postulate rafts, canoes or primitive sailing ships as vehicles for an Atlantic crossing, we must accept that the goal of the journey was known in advance.

I do not underestimate the courage in undertaking bold ventures shown by our ancestors just out of the Stone Age, I even credit them with audacity in times of peril, but not with a penchant for suicide. As land-lubbers they were certainly afraid of the stormy seas which could crush their miserable rafts like nutshells. But if they did risk the perilous expedition, they must have been sure of a worthwhile goal. If we admit that, the question WHY becomes pretty clear. The 'gods' promised them a blessed country far, far away! This promise made it necessary for them to instruct their protégés in the arts of ship-building, navigation, etc. They showed the small groups of people — it was not a mass migration — the route to the goal. Just as it says in the traditions.

There remains the speculation about what reason the 'gods' may have had for the distribution of small groups of people in various parts of the world. Were they concerned with training their semi-divine offspring in new, safe territories? Did they foresee in outline the future evolution of humanity, the direction the further development of their intelligence would take? Lastly, did they expect that among the progeny of the artificially produced Noah and Melchizedek there might be scientists who would find and understand the 'divine' legacy? Were they sure that the trails they laid could never be lost?

Living creatures are subject to certain patterns of behaviour whether they like it or not. At night mosquitoes fly towards the light: they cannot help it. Man must eat and drink in order to live, whether it suits him or not. These are vital functions of the organism.

Intelligent reason asks questions whether it wants to or not. Intelligence wants to know what it was like in the past and how we became what we are. Who originated the idea that *homo sapiens* is different from animals? This series of intelligent questions leads unerringly back to the 'gods', whether we like it or not. Intelligent questioning can only be temporarily interrupted by fake answers; it suddenly finds itself dissatisfied with half-truths. Intelligence is an untameable beast. It keeps on asking what things were like in the past. And in the end it realises that the history of mankind without the 'gods' leads into a landscape, the map of which is blank.

Myth and legend are impregnated with the enormous impression the 'gods' made on primitive man. Chroniclers

Joseph Smith (1805–44), the founder of the Church of Jesus Christ of Latter-day Saints.

Imaginative painting of the vision of Moroni, the heavenly messenger.

Salt Lake Temple · W00133

The Mormon Temple in Salt Lake City.

The village square of Chavín de Huantar.

The road led upwards through a rust-coloured gorge in a series of acute hairpin bends.

picked up the red thread of tradition and spun it further. That is how the 'divine' deeds were recorded, down from their thunderous arrival to the manifold didactic instructions to the inhabitants of the earth. With their abilities our early ancestors transformed what they had learnt into architectonic master-pieces, made use of 'anachronistic' technology and created amazing objects of art.

The Popol Vuh, one of the great books from the dawn of mankind, shows how deliberately the trails were laid. It says that the servants of God 'brought the writings of Tula across the sea. They called the scripture that wherein their history was written.' The ancient traditions of the Quiché Maya refer to yet older writings and part of the Book of Mormon consisted of such writings. Joseph Smith translated the crossing of the Atlantic by the Jaredites from the 24 plates of the Book of Mormon, which form only the smallest part.

Smith translated most of the book from the plate called Nephi. Who was Nephi? He was the son of a Jewish family who lived in Jerusalem around 600 BC, i.e. thousands of years after the Jaredites. His father was called Lehi, his mother Sariah.

In chapter 1, verse 4 of the Book of Mormon, Nephi writes:

For it came to pass in the commencement of the first year of the reign of Zedekiah, king of Judah ... there came many prophets prophesying unto the people that they must repent, or the great city of Jerusalem must be destroyed.

That is right. Jerusalem was completely destroyed in 586 BC. Jeremiah and Ezekiel were prominent in this legendary age. It must have been a special period, for both prophets spoke incessantly with their 'God', who descended from heaven in fire-breathing chariots that made a frightening noise.

Nephi's father Lehi repeated the experiences of the prophets, as is described in Nephi, 1.6 et seq.:

And it came to pass as he prayed unto the Lord, there came a pillar of fire and dwelt upon a rock before him ... he saw one [an angel] descending out of the midst of heaven, and he beheld that his lustre was above that of the sun at noon-day.

The being from the pillar of fire ordered Lehi to assemble

Sariah, his sons and daughters (Nephi being among them), and friends of the family in order to inform them that they were destined to travel to a distant country. After initial difficulties, the migrant group built a ship under the guidance of the mysterious Lord: 'And it came to pass that the Lord spake unto me, saying: Thou shalt construct a ship, after the manner *which I shall show thee, that I may carry thy people across the water* (1 Nephi 17.8).

As if that was not enough, the mysterious alien gave the ship-builders special astronauts' food which needed neither preparation nor cooking. He knew that eating keeps body and soul together, but also that another object was even more important — a compass!

> And it came to pass that as my father arose in the morning, and went forth to the tent door, to his great astonishment he beheld upon the ground a round ball of curious workmanship. And within the ball were two spindles; and the one pointed the way whither we should go into the wilderness . . . And we did follow the directions of the ball, which led us in the more fertile parts of the wilderness.

Father Lehi died during the crossing. Nephi assumed command. Nephi's brothers were jealous because of the special favour the 'Lord' showed him and they tied him to a ship's beam. In this tricky situation, they found out how indispensable the compass was. 'And it came to pass that after they had bound me insomuch that I could not move, the compass, which been prepared of the Lord, did cease to work.'

The Mutiny on the Bounty came to an end and the expedition reached the American continent, with the metal plates and the compass: 'Now I, Nephi, had also brought the records which were engraven upon the plates of brass; and also the ball or compass, which was prepared for my father by the hand of the Lord.' (II Nephi 5.12).

Following Nephi's account, Mormon scholars are convinced that the group first wandered from the Red Sea through the Arabian peninsula, then built their ship on the coast of the Indian Ocean, somewhere in the area of the Gulf of Aden and Oman, and finally reached the coast of South America across the South Pacific. James E. Talmage (19) puts this around 590 BC, a date we should take note of.

There is one amazing coincidence. The translation that Joseph Smith made from the metal plates in 1827 is duplicated in the Popol Vuh. But Smith could not possibly have known the contents of the Quiché Maya bible, for it was only translated for the first time by Wolfgang Gordan in the 1950s!

Two groups reached the American continent independently of each other. First, the Jaredites in their hermetically sealed ships in the age of the first wave of the gods. It was the legendary epoch in which flourished the chroniclers of Adam's sapphire book, Enoch's ascent into heaven, the test-tube babies Noah and Melchizedek, as well as the 'lords' of creation Utnapishtim, Ziusudra and others. Secondly, the Nephites, who set out from the east and reached South America thousands of years later, around 590 BC.

Soon after the landing Nephi had a temple built:

And I, Nephi, did build a temple; and I did construct it after the manner of the temple of Solomon save it were not built of so many precious things. But the manner of the construction was like unto the temple of Solomon; and the workmanship thereof was exceeding fine.

(II Nephi 5.16)

It is not my concern to prove which parts of the Book of Mormon are genuine, but it may please the followers of the Church of Jesus Christ of Latter-day Saints that one proof emerges as a by-product of my researches.

Nephi built a temple 'after the manner of the temple of Solomon'. In so far as this information is valid, South America must contain a temple (on a smaller scale) of the kind Solomon had built in Jerusalem — a complex with outer and inner courts, a sanctuary with a temple which had four doors aligned on the four cardinal points of the compass. This temple must have originated between the fifth and sixth centuries BC.

Moreover, Nephi's temple must have been built 'cold', so to speak, without prototypes or borrowings from typical South American architecture. The temple must have been the first of its kind, an edifice that appeared out of the blue without local traditions.

I am not only on the trail of a temple which meets these pre-requisites, I am also on the trail of the 'Lord' who led the Nephites to South America. Did this 'god' still exist after the landing or had he transformed himself into spirit? Also, where did Nephi recruit the large numbers of builders needed? After all, he arrived with only a small group. 'Immediately after their arrival, the Nephites began ... to till the earth, and we began to plant seeds: yea, we did plant all the seeds which we had brought from the land of Jerusalem' (I Nephi 18.24).

The Nephites produced progeny assiduously, for they practised polygamy (forbidden to the Mormons by government decree in 1890). Assuming that the immigrant group consisted of 100 men and 100 women, and each woman bore one child a year, the Nephites would have numbered 1,500 souls in 15 years. The firstborn, pubescent teenagers of 15 followed the example of their elders and willingly played their part in multiplying. In 30 years a good 5,000 Nephites would praise their 'Lord'. Quite enough people to build the temple, especially as there were indigenous workers to collaborate with them. The personnel was there.

The Lord was present! As soon as he arrived, he gave Nephi this task: 'And it came to pass that the Lord commanded me, wherefore I did make plates of ore that I might engraven upon them the record of my people' (I Nephi 19.1).

Thirty years later. The 'Lord' set great store by a complete log book. Once again he ordered Nephi:

And thirty years had passed away from the time we left Jerusalem. And it came to pass that the Lord God said unto me: Make other plates; and thou shalt engraven many things upon them which are good in my sight, for the profit of thy people.

Was the 'Lord' vain? Why did he want the 'Things ... which are good in my sight' noted down? The 'Lord' constantly insisted upon his golden words being engraved upon the metal plates. He considered them important for the future, otherwise he would have had them recorded on perishable materials such as papyrus, leather or wood. This 'Lord' in his wisdom took care that his communications, addressed to intelligent beings in the future, were permanent.

A difficult question. Is there a temple in South America modelled on Solomon's masterpiece? Is there some proof of the activities of the gods to be found there?

I invite you to visit that temple.

2 In the Beginning Everything Was Different

> Drawing the attention of the masses to something means putting healthy human reason on the right track.'
>
> Gotthold Ephraim Lessing (1729–81)

The Jerusalem of the Andes is called Chavín de Huantar.

It was raining cats and dogs on that April day in 1980 when two young missionaries, soaked to the skin, stood outside the door of our house in Feldbrunnen. The older one, about 30 years old, was an American called Charlie, the younger man's name was Paul and he came from Berne. My visitors from the Church of Jesus Christ of Latter-day Saints made me a present of the German version of the Book of Mormon. (I already had seven other translations in my library.) I invited the missionaries to come inside to warm up and drink a cup of coffee.

My fellow countryman Paul asked what I thought of the Book of Mormon. I said that I found the plates Ether and Nephi exciting and informative. Nor did I think they were forgeries, but found it unfortunate that some rather crude prophecies about Jesus had been added to the original text.

Naturally, the young missionaries disagreed with me. Either the complete Book of Mormon was inspired by the Holy Ghost and therefore 'genuine', or the whole book was worthless. Being well up in the subject, I showed my disinclination for a discussion that would lead nowhere, a hint that was very quickly taken by Paul, belying the reputation the Bernese have for being slow-witted. He asked, 'You know many ruins in South America. Have you found any that resemble Solomon's temple in Jerusalem?'

I told him truthfully that I had not. The missionaries said goodbye without trying to make a hopeless conversion. It was such a terrible April day that they would certainly have found a willing victim if they could have promised me blue skies.

Paul, the Bernese, had put a bee in my bonnet which went on buzzing, but another one was tormenting me even more.

Whether the temple mentioned in the Book of Nephi existed in South America or not seemed far less important to me than the question whether the temple described in detail by the prophet Ezekiel in the Old Testament existed — a temple in a distant land, standing on a high mountain, built like the temple of Solomon. If there were a temple in South America that fitted Ezekiel's description, that *would be* a thrilling story.

What has the Nephi of the Book of Mormon to do with the Ezekiel of the Bible? Well, both of them lived at the same time in the same geographical zone. Perhaps they knew each other. Both of them wrote about a flying god who came down and gave instructions. On this god's orders, Nephi had a temple built in South America and Ezekiel was flown by the same god to a distant land where he was shown a temple on the Solomonic model on a 'very high mountain'.

It is established that Ezekiel lived in Jerusalem and Babylon. If someone showed him the temple in South America — he describes it incredibly accurately — someone must have flown him there and then back to the Near East. There is no other possibility.

So my search for a Solomonic temple in South America was by no means purely inspired by the Book of Mormon, I was also looking for Ezekiel's temple and the trail of the 'flying god', who was at the back of it all. I only realised much later that both trails would meet in the most fascinating way.

My eyes were aching from looking at an endless procession of temples in books on archaeology. At the time finding *the* temple meant more to me than the sight of a blue Mauritius means to a philatelist. If I suspected similarities, the plan of Solomon's temple in Jerusalem told me that essential details were missing, that it was too early or too old, or that it did not belong to the period of Nephi or Ezekiel. I went through 39 lavishly illustrated books. In all of them Chavín de Huantar was described. I decided to visit this site, take accurate measurements and see the landscape in which it lies with my own eyes.

Nineteen eighty-one. Once again Europe was enjoying a cold wet spring. It was autumn in Peru when I rented a kind of Russian jeep, a Lada Niva, in Lima, the capital.

Long before dawn, I was driving along a smooth asphalt road, the Panamericana del Norte, one of the best roads in the world, through sandy desert bordering the coast in the direction of Trujillo, the fourth largest city in Peru. I left the Panamericana at the town of Pativilca. After that sugar-cane plantations lined the road.

When I was handing over 200 soles at a toll station, a horrible stench from the Lada Niva assailed my nostrils. The cap of the petrol tank was missing. I wrapped a piece of plastic round a stone and blocked the stinking hole with it.

After running for 30 km through a stony desert, past the menacing spurs of the mountains, the road began to climb gradually. After turning off from Pativilca — in the distance you can see the ruins of a fortress from the time of the Chimu Indians — I reached the God-forsaken village of Chas-quitambo at a height of 780 m. In ancient times this place was a handing-over point for Inca relay runners. Nowadays, too, the best thing is to keep on running.

The ascent into a rust-coloured gorge began in a series of acute hairpin bends. The lowering rain clouds now lay behind me, the fog banks cleared and opened up a panorama of light brown and black mountains.

My clattering Russian banger was becoming less willing with every curve. On the narrow road, my red star could no longer make it in second gear. Near Cajacay, at a height of 2,600 m, the old fellow was completely out of breath. Automobile asthma. The engine needed more oxygen. I unscrewed the top of the air filter. The filter which was supposed to let the air through felt like the remains of a plaster cast. I threw it away, screwed the top on to the empty filter, started and the old jalopy leapt forward. It had understood me. It *had* to get me up the mountain.

After every hairpin bend I hoped I had reached the top of the pass. For a long time these were vain hopes, for more and more mountain valleys kept appearing. The clay huts by the roadside became fewer. Indians in colourful ponchos, carrying heavy bundles on their backs, put one foot before the other in the steady rhythm of the experienced mountain climber. I was amazed that the hard-working local inhabitants could scratch a living from the sterile rocky soil up here, yet a third of Peru's 14.6 million inhabitants live in these uplands.

I reached the cloud-filled pass at a height of 4,100 m. In European latitudes it would have been a zone of permanent ice and snow, but Peru is closer to the Equator. Only dry grasses and miserable stunted bushes grow up here.

A young dark-brown Indian woman, with a baby on her breast in a cloth bag and a heavy sack of potatoes on her back, looked at me suspiciously when I asked her if she would like a lift, because friendly foreigners are rare in this region. I took the sack off her back and pushed it behind the seats of the Lada Niva. She got in and laughed self-consciously after arranging the six skirts that all Indian women wear. We drove past the frozen lagoon of Conocochca with the glaciers of the 6,600 m high Cordillera de Huyauhuish ahead of us.

I managed to worm out of the taciturn Indian woman where she was going — the town of Catac at a height of 3,540 m in the valley of the Rio Santa. I shuddered at the idea of the woman having to walk the 40 km stretch with her heavy burdens — it would have taken her two days, but we did it in half an hour. In Catac the road forks off to Chavín de Huantar.

At the only petrol station I filled my jeep with a young woman and two men. She was called Ruth; Uri and Isaac had black and red beards respectively. They were Israelis who had decided to roam through the world for a year with no fixed plans, although they did not exclude visits to archaeological sites like Chavín de Huantar. They asked why I was going there. I limited myself to vague remarks about a Solomonic temple connected with the prophet Ezekiel. They might be the sort of fanatically orthodox Israelis who would have been shocked by the real object of my research.

'Are you Swiss?' asked Uri. 'Then you must know Erich von Däniken's books. I am not sure whether the ideas he puts forward are crazy or rational.'

Instead of answering I bit my lip.

Beyond Catac the road was not asphalted and led in tortuous curves to the picturesque icy lake of Quericocha at a height of 3,980 m. The snowclad summit of Yanamarey (5,260 m) caught the eye.

Next came the tunnel through the Kahuish pass (4,510 m). The word 'tunnel' might call up false associations with the tunnels in Western industrial countries but I should point out that this 500 m long specimen is only hacked roughly out of the rock with an unmade road, full of potholes, running through it. Icy water drips from roof and walls and there are no

lights or signals in the one track nightmare road. If the head-
lights of an oncoming car appear, the driver nearest the exit
or entrance has to back out. Naturally, everyone drives in the
hope of not meeting an oncoming car in the dark hole. This
tunnel does not deserve a star in the guide books.

If the uphill drive had been taxing, the steep descent on the
other side of the tunnel into the Mosna valley proved really
frightening, even for a veteran driver like me. The narrow unmade road winds like an endless snake clinging to the
mountain in curve after curve. Your eyes cling to the left
because a sheer abyss threatens on the right. We reached the
bottom of the valley at the little village of Machac (3,180 m).
The ruins of Chavín de Huantar are clearly visible, close to the
road.

The Hotel Turistas was full to the last bed, not of tourists
but archaeologists. We met the crème de la crème of German
and Peruvian archaeologists. In the distinguished German
group, Professors Udo Oberem and Henning Bischof greeted
me politely, and their Peruvian colleagues were polite and
friendly. To the Germans I am an unpredictable outsider,
always planning some new trick. The Peruvians have a
different opinion of me. When I was honoured by the aldermen
of the town of Nazca some years ago, the mayor said in his
address that there were many theories about the lines on the
plain of Nazca. He could not say whether they were a calendar
or a take-off point for hot-air balloons, the remains of Inca
roads, magical signs, the marking lines of a sportsground or
landmarks for extraterrestrials. 'As for those of who live and
work here,' said the mayor, 'we are not primarily interested
which of the experts is right. But one thing is certain: Herr von
Däniken has brought the most tourists to our region!'

Over the evening meal the Israelis asked if they could help
me in any way, for they had found out who had given them
a lift. I accepted their offer gratefully, for a continuity girl
was just what I needed when taking my measurements.

In the morning the Israelis were waiting for me on a sunny
hill outside the site of the ruins. They were suitably draped
in cameras and measuring apparatus. We passed through the
massive wooden gate into the ruins of Chavín de Huantar.

The section of the complex that is still preserved is called
El Castillo, the castle, although it never was a castle. It is a

IN THE BEGINNING EVERYTHING WAS DIFFERENT

rectangular building 72.90 m long and 70 m wide. Large granite blocks, fitting together to the millimetre, form the rectangular façades. The lower monoliths nearest to the ground are the best preserved. The higher the building, which slopes slightly inwards, rises, the more clearly visible are the ravages of time — just like the Solomonic temple in Jerusalem which suffered 36 wars and was destroyed 17 times. At Chavín as in Jerusalem new walls were built each time on the lower blocks of stone.

The main portal of the Castillo faces east, the direction of the sunrise (and Jerusalem). Two columns, topped by a monolith nine metres long, are flanked by square and rectangular granite slabs. The squat columns are decorated with incomprehensible patterns in relief, as are the crowning monolith and the adjacent slabs. Weathering through the ages has worn down the reliefs and unfortunately man, too, has damaged the delicate work. When El Castillo first stood there in all its glory, the massive structure must have looked like a single, almost seamless block, even from a short distance. El Castillo was the termination and crown of the temple complex, the Holy of Holies, to which only the high priests had access.

Today a rubbish heap overgrown with clumps of grass is concealed behind the main portal. A few steps lower down lies a square which occupies the whole width of the Castillo — the forecourt of the sanctuary. Some 36 m from the Castillo, more steps lead down to a second gigantic courtyard (70 by 42 m), from which yet more steps lead to the so-called 'sunken square' (the length of the sides are 49.70 m).

To the north and south of the sunken square rise platforms, which have not yet been excavated, but you can recognise the artificial hill by the scattered monoliths protruding from it. The whole site is reckoned to cover an area of some 13 hectares, but so far only the temple complex has been excavated. It is known that the whole layout stood on a man-made stone platform.

Four flights of steps lead from the sunken square to the four cardinal points of the compass with absolute accuracy, as I checked with my own compass. The side of the plateau descends 80 m to the bed of the River Mosna which flows past the temple in a south-easterly direction.

The complex measures 228 m from the western wall of the Castillo to the south-east corner. The section excavated to date is about 175 m wide. These measurements do not include the wall that once enclosed the area. Remains of this wall are visible on the west side.

At all events, a huge rectangular complex stood here with outer and inner courtyards and the (still extant) ten-metre-high Holy of Holies, with inner and outer courtyards for the priests and the people. The rectangle is aligned on the four cardinal points of the compass with its steps and doors and the main portal points to the east, exactly like the Solomonic temple in Jerusalem.

Today Solomon's temple in Jerusalem no longer forms an exact rectangle; it is now an irregular trapezoid, with sides of 315 m to the north, 280 m to the south, 485 m to the west and 470 m to the east (1). However, the original temple was strictly rectangular. King Herod was responsible for the distorted shape, which doubled the area, and because the space was lacking, additional supporting walls were built on which (in those days) new platforms were placed.

Ruth, Uri and Isaac were busy measuring the courtyards, walls and monoliths, while I was taking photographs from every angle and in every corner. When we stopped for a cigarette and Ruth showed me my notepad clipped to a board, I held my breath. This was professional work! With delicate lines she had drawn a site plan that was ready for the printers. All the walls and monoliths, the steps and flights of stairs and the sunken square were sketched in. The beginning and end of the lines were marked by small arrows to show which sections the measurements referred to.

We sat on boulders, which were not in short supply. I asked my new friends what their jobs were. Ruth said drily, 'I am a surveyor for road building and land measurement.'

So that accounted for the professionalism! Uri turned out to be a teacher, Isaac a pilot. The gods had put the right team into my Lada Niva! The four of us did a job which would have taken me four times as long by myself.

Together we explored the network of passages and galleries under Chavín de Huantar. One passage on the east side of the main square was only 1.10 m high and 67 cm wide and it was impossible to stand upright in it. For one very good reason.

On 17 January 1945 Chavín de Huantar was swamped by

a massive flood. It happened like this. The little river Mosna runs past the south-east side; on the north-west side, between the ruins and the Indian village of Chavin, a stream called Huacheqsa tumbles down into the depths. It rises from a mountain lake which is fed by the water melting from a glacier in the cordillera. In December 1944 and January 1945 more water flowed in than the lake could take and the rocky banks broke like a dam. The stream became a raging torrent and covered the low-lying parts of Chavín de Huantar with a dark brown layer of mud which penetrated the underground passages. When the waters subsided, scree, sand and mud were left behind.

The passage through which I crawled with the help of a flashlight was once higher, or deeper, whichever you prefer. When I had gone as far as I could in the passage beneath the ruins, I saw five lateral tunnels, 60 cm high and 48 cm wide. They may have formed part of an irrigation system, especially as the main passage ran in the direction of the river Mosna.

However, as a 1.72 cm high passage on the west side ran in a southerly direction, i.e. not in the direction of a stream, the subterranean infrastructure cannot have been intended to act solely as water mains.

Chavín de Huantar had been flooded in earlier times. In 1919 the Peruvian archaeologist Julio C. Tello carried out extensive excavations with a group of Indians. When he returned in 1934, the stream had 'destroyed part of the main wing' (2). Tello writes that a third of the complex which he had seen when it was still intact was then destroyed and that many subterranean passages and channels had been flushed out. Kilometres away Tello found stone, metal, and pottery artefacts on a sandbank in the river miles from the temple. They had been swept out of the temple ruins.

When the temple first stood there in all its glory, the raging mountain torrents could not have affected it. The closely fitting megalithic walls were watertight, the irrigation channels around and under Chavín de Huantar functioned and the streams were under control. It was only when fallen trees and monoliths hindered the flow of the water and after grave robbers cut holes in the walls of the Castillo that the water could exercise its destructive power on the buildings.

Together we set out to explore the passages which run under Chavín de Huantar in a tortuous network.

The next day my Israelis took a local bus in which the passengers were packed like sardines. I promised I would send them all a copy of my book in Hebrew, with a personal dedication. We had only spent two days together, yet I missed Ruth and the bearded men when I drove my Lada Niva back to the ruins to take a closer look at the passages in the rubbish dump.

Two tunnels on the north side of the Castillo are shut off by iron grilles to stop tourists going into the dark labyrinth on their own. And it is a labyrinth, as I found out.

Just beyond the entrance the first tunnel leads to a remarkable stele, *El Lanzon*, the lance or spear. *El Lanzon* is situated at the intersection of the two passages which are over three metres high, but only 50 cm wide. Monolithic granite slabs form the ceiling.

In spite of its strange proportions, this passage would be hardly worth mentioning if it did not contain an inexplicable puzzle. *El Lanzon* is a giant stele more than four metres high, yet the passages are little more than three metres high. How did *El Lanzon* get here? It is not a rubber giant that could have been bent. Given its great length, it could not have been manoeuvred horizontally around the countless bends in the 50 cm wide passage. There is only one solution. Right from the start, the architects of Chavín de Huantar planned an opening in the ceiling through which the stele could be lowered into the crossing between the two passages, before the rest of the vast temple complex was erected over it.

No one knows how to interpret *El Lanzon*. The Czecho-slovakian archaeologist and ethnologist Miloslav Stingl (3) describes the stele as:

A very strange creature. Large jaguar teeth stick out over the lower lip. The eyes are staring upwards as if they were looking up to heaven. The belt round the god's body is also decorated with jaguar heads. Two snake heads hang from the belt. The god holds his right hand up, the other rests on his hip.

That is a description, not an interpretation, and I find it hard even to follow the description because I cannot recognise a 'creature' in *El Lanzon* at all. True, you can make out a

The stele El Lanzon is situated deep underground at the crossing of the two passages. It is more than three metres high, but only 50 cm wide.

El Lanzon is lavishly adorned with ornaments. No one knows what they mean. There are many explanations, but none which makes sense.

big muzzle with protruding 'jaguar teeth', but not in the place where jaguars normally have their fatal fangs. Where Miloslav Stingl sees jaguar teeth, I recognise — equally imaginatively — joints of armour, since *El Lanzon* strikes me as a technical artefact rather than an animal figure.

Apart from the passage through which I came to confront *El Lanzon*, all the passages leading from the intersection come to a dead end. After a few paces I was halted by massive walls. That struck me as odd. What was the sense of the planners of Chavín de Huantar only completing the passage to *El Lanzon*, and ending all the other tunnels in a mysterious full stop? All that work for an architectural joke? I suspected secret doors behind the dead ends of the passages. No more and no less.

As I could go no farther, I retraced my steps. Outside the sun was blinding as it can only be in the clear air at a height

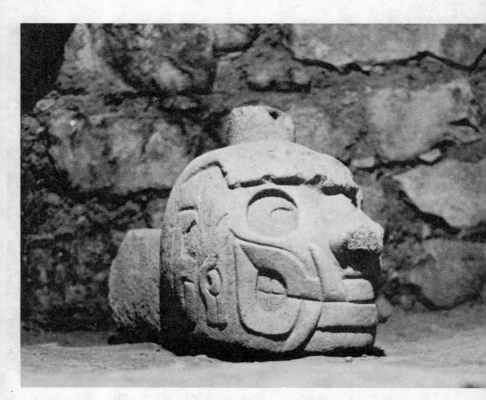

A menacing helmeted figure blocked my way.

of 3,000 m. I blinked hard and entered the second tunnel which runs southwards under the Castillo. It was lit by weak bulbs along the walls and they suddenly failed. I groped my way back into the daylight. A friendly attendant lent me an old-fashioned carbide lamp. (I gave him my lighter as surety and I was soon to miss it.) The smell reminded me for a moment of my first bicycle.

The harsh light shone on passages three metres high and cut out of the rock, and on the monoliths forming the ceiling. Soon the tunnel branched off to the left and right; I chose the left-hand one.

I nearly fell over a stone head which, at first glance, looked like a helmeted being, possibly humanoid. In the past the walls were covered with reliefs depicting winged figures flying upwards. Today only vestiges remain as evidence. The figures are carved with such delicacy and in such low relief that they might have been made by a modern dentist using a high-speed drill to practise his hobby of sculpting. But nowadays dentists have no time for badly paid hobbies, they prefer to invest in lucrative high-rise buildings. This passage also came to a dead-end formed by a massive wall.

With all the zeal and patience of a Boy Scout, I went back to the main passage, tried a different entrance, climbed seven steep steps and reached another corridor. It was 1.30 m wide and 1.83 m high. Two people could comfortably walk side by side in it. Across the top of the steps ran a narrower passage with three exits leading to three chambers 5.70 m long, 1.94 m wide and 2.25 m high. The harsh light of the carbide lamp revealed grotesque figures. Strange stone heads revealed their helmets and gave me haughty, rather mocking looks. They were asking, 'What do you think of us?'

Many times I tried to find a way through the walls, but could not manage it. I trotted back to the central corridor, made two 90-degree turns on my own axis and entered another room. In it stone heads were neatly arranged on a wooden plank facing reliefs showing all kinds of fabulous scenes. How many more passages and chambers await excavation? Perhaps the secret of the 'gods' awaits discovery deep below the ruins, perhaps the architects preserved the key to the misinterpreted culture of Chavín de Huantar deep underground?

While I scrutinised every square inch of the wall which closed

There are also easily accessible passages — a good 1.80 metres high and 1.30 metres wide.

Deep in the earth stone heads with strange faces stared at me in the harsh light of the carbide lamp.

off the tunnel to see if there was any trace of an opening, the carbide lamp gave up the ghost. I was in darkness. It was as quiet as the grave. For the first time I felt a draught of cold air passing through the chambers. Although I could not see, I felt my way to the source of the draught, stumbling over stone heads and bumping into monoliths. I took several flash-light photos, as I had plenty of batteries. The current of air came from under the floor of the rear wall. Was there a passage behind it leading even deeper into the earth? I fingered the masonry, pulling hard on protruding parts of the blocks, but nothing budged.

I cautiously put one foot ahead of the other, taking flash photos. I sadly missed the lighter I had left with the attendant.

I crawled upwards on all fours.

One passage wall felt much like another; none of them gave a clue where to go. I had to find the stairway whose seven steps I had climbed up and now must climb down again. But the stairway I felt led upwards. The current of air grew stronger along the walls. I crawled upwards on all fours. Another seven steps and I saw light right above me. The tunnel led beneath an iron grille which could easily be lifted up. I hauled myself out of the depths into the open air and tried to decide where I was.

I had come out of the labyrinth roughly in the centre of the Castillo, high above the east-facing main entrance. The huge rectangle of the temple complex spread out below me. I clambered down and sat down under the main gate to catch my breath. I looked up to try to find out which hole I had crawled out of . . . and discovered strange flying creatures engraved on the underside of the monolith lying across the columns.

They consisted of 14 cherubs, as the Bible calls the watchers of the heavens. Seven figures resembling birds of prey were looking northwards and seven southwards. It struck me that all the stairways I had ascended or descended had seven steps. Was the 'sacred number seven' the number giving the key to Chavín de Huantar?

The number seven has traditions which are not confined to the seven-year itch. Its magic is invoked in the seven-day periods into which the month is divided. Around 1,600 BC the Babylonians did away with their five-day week and introduced the seven-day week. In the seven celestial bodies, Sun, Moon, Mercury, Venus, Mars, Jupiter and Saturn, the Babylonians saw the whole order of the cosmos. Among the Jews, the seven days of creation and the seven-branched menorah of the tabernacle testify to the importance of the sacred seven. In the Revelation of St John we find the 'book with seven seals'. Seven has significance in Buddhism and Malayan civilisation. In ancient Greece seven days of grace were common. Thebes had its famous seven gates, there were seven wise men ... and then there were the seven wonders of the world. Was the number seven revered in Chavín de Huantar, too?

No code is safe to our modern intelligence services. Surely it should be possible to crack codes that are simply begging for decipherment?

Down below one 'sunken square' a collaborator of the archaeologist Julio C. Tello found an obelisk that today stands in the Archaeological Museum of Lima. It is called the Tello obelisk and its sign language awaits interpretation. I spent hours in front of it, taking photographs and copying the engravings on it. I asked Peruvian archaeologists about the possible meaning of the patterns. I soon realised that they knew nothing definite when they struck up the cult aria: the jaguar cult, the bird of prey cult, etc. I could equally well sing the pyramid cult, as small pyramids can also be made out on the Tello obelisk. Down below the square where the obelisk was found stands the 'Altar of the Seven Goats' (also known as the 'Altar of the Constellation Orion'). My zoological imagination was not powerful enough to make out seven goats, but the arrangement of seven holes in the altar does correspond approximately to the position of the seven satellites in the constellation of Orion.

The Tello obelisk.

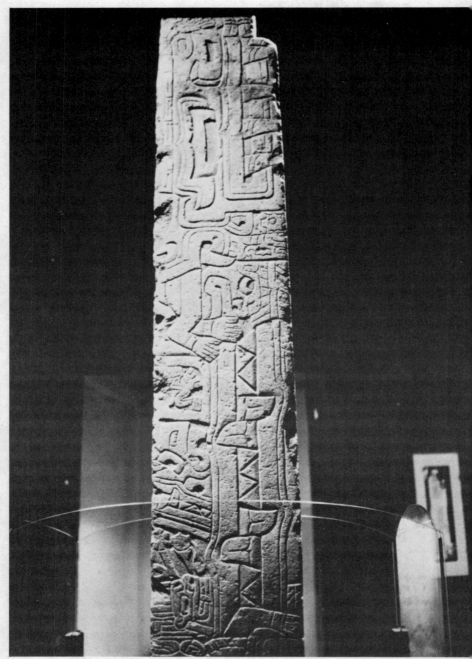

Today the Tello obelisk from Chavin de Huantar is housed in the Archaeological Museum at Lima. The engraved ornamentation with its bewildering interplay of images has not yet been 'deciphered'.

or insect cult among the Colombian Indians. Besides, the model aircraft do not have fish or insect heads.

The Gold Museum was well worth my second visit. The thousands of exhibits stimulate the imagination and make one admire the ancient Indian artists. They take one far back into the world of puzzles and mysteries, the world which was so ruthlessly ended by the Spanish conquerors.

That evening my patience snapped. Dr Forero is a kind, helpful and reliable man and I did not doubt for a moment that he was making great efforts on my behalf. Over dinner he explained to me that many of the air force officers whom Colonel Baer-Ruiz wanted to invite were away on courses or commandos and that he did not want me to lecture to a tiny audience. Dreaded *mañana* was rearing its head.

Dr Forero suggested in all earnest that I should stay in the country for another three months. A big UFO congress was due to take place in Bogotá in August and the organisers would be delighted for me to lecture. And during that time I would certainly be able to achieve my aim of visiting the lost city in the jungle. *Mañana*.

I had allowed one week for this excursion in my travel plans, after that I had contracted to give lectures in Germany, Austria and Switzerland as part of my programme for the year.

'I'm going to fly to Santa Marta and try to find my own way into the jungle,' I said. Dr Foreero advised against this.

If the army had cordoned off the excavation zone, not even a Colombian, let alone a foreigner, could reach it.

I thanked Dr Forero warmly for all his help and said I was sure we should meet again.

The next day I flew back to Switzerland.

5   *The Eighth Wonder of the World*

'The question today is how we can persuade mankind to agree
to its own survival.'

Bertrand Russell (1872–1970)

Before my departure I had booked a room in the Hilton for
14 August. At the end of July I confirmed with Dr Forero
that I would attend the congress in Bogotá, but added that
my main reason for coming was to meet Professor Soto and
visit the lost city.

Lufthansa flight 512 landed punctually at 21.40 hours on
the rain-soaked landing strip at Bogotá. Was I dreaming? Had
nearly three months passed since I had flown away from here
in frustration? The certainty that I would now be able to see
the lost city delighted me.

My booking was confirmed at the Hilton, the youthful head
of reception told me, but there was no room available. Furious
because it was night, I was tired and no other accommodation
would be available, I tried the old joke.

Putting on my most serious face, I asked, 'Would you have
had a room for Queen Elizabeth if she had arrived unexpectedly?'

The young man looked at me with a wild surmise. 'Well,'
he said perplexedly, 'in that case we would have to make an
exception.'

'Give me the Queen's room. I promise you she won't arrive
tonight.'

The man in the black suit had no sense of humour. He
refused to offer me one of the rooms which all hotels of this
category keep in reserve. After one last question: 'So you've
no room for me?' I began to open my bags so that I could
lie down on a sofa in the hall. Why should I suffer for a
blunder by the staff? I was worn out after the flight and the
resultant jet lag; I longed for a bed. Worried about my
imminent striptease, the young man summoned the manager

and of course he had a room for me. Why couldn't I have had one straight away?

At nine o'clock the next morning I was woken from a long refreshing sleep. Dr Forero was on the line.

'So you're here. I can't believe it!'

'But we did arrange to meet today.'

I had arrived before my letter written at the end of July. We met an hour later. Apart from three lectures in the Teatro Libertador, I was to address the Rotarians on two evenings and also give the talk which Colonel Baer-Ruiz had planned during my last visit.

'What news of Professor Soto?'

Miguel Forero was prepared for my question and took a book from his briefcase entitled *Buritaca 200 (Ciudad Perdida)*, the Lost City (1). The author: Professor Soto Holguin. I flicked through it. Flights of steps overhung with lianas, moss-covered walls, terraces in the midst of luxuriant virgin forest.

'Fastastic,' I said, 'and what about Soto?'

'If it suits you, you can meet him at the University at eleven o'clock tomorrow morning.'

It is easy to find one's way about in the big city. Bogotá is covered by a network of streets intersecting at right angles. All the streets running from north to south are called *carreras*, except for occasional grandiose *avenidas*. The streets which cross the *carreras* at right angles are called *calles* and like the larger streets running from north to south they are numbered consecutively.

I arrived punctually at eleven o'clock at Professor Soto's Institute on Carrera No. 1. The tall slim archaeologist greeted me with a smile.

'So you're the man who writes those books!'

'Do you think I shouldn't?' I countered.

'Not at all. Science is open to all opinions.'

So the professor, quite young to hold a chair at the age of 38, was prepared to accept views outside the standard dogmas. I admired him as a rare example of his profession.

In an auditorium we sat in chairs with an arm rest on the right so that the students could take notes. The professor lolled on the seat and puffed at a cigarette. I asked: 'You call the lost city Buritaca 200. What does that mean?'

'The Sierra Nevada of Santa Marta extends between 32° 50′

Professor Alvaro Soto Holguin received me at his institute in the university for our first conversation.

and 74° 15′ west of Greenwich. Latitudinally the region comprises latitudes of 10° 5′ and 11° 20′ situated north of the Equator. Several small rivers have their sources in this region and some of them flow into the Caribbean in north-westerly direction. One of them is the Rio Buritaca, on the banks of which the "Lost City" is located. Hence Buritaca 200.'

'But what does the number 200 mean?'

'It is the two hundredth settlement, the two hundredth city, so to speak, that we have located so far.'

'It sound incredible. Does that mean that the whole jungle area was once dotted with settlements and urban cultures?'

'Yes, the area is enormous. You can form a rough idea of it when I tell you that we already know more than 2,000 kilometres of roads and tracks with stone surfaces. We have been excavating since 1976 and there is no end in sight. Buritaca 200 alone is ten times as big as the famous Inca fortress of Macchu Picchu in Peru.'

A girl student served us coffee. Colombian coffee tastes good all over the world, but it is never made so strong as in its home country. It would be interesting to know whether the Colombians all have heart disease or whether they hardly know where their hearts are beating because of the coffee. I asked; 'When was the city built and by whom?'

'On the basis of previous datings using the radioactive carbon isotope carbon 14, we conclude that Buritaca 200 was built around AD 800. The builders were the Tairona Indians, a sub-group of the Chibcha. Scholars also speak of a Tairona culture, but that is absurd, because the Tairona did not use that name for themselves. It was the Spaniards who gave the name to the Indians living in the Sierra Nevada. Not such a strange name when you know that the word *tairo* means something like 'casting metal' and the gold-hungry conquerors were only out after metal.'

'Did you find pottery or graves with mummies in?'

'We found ceramics and some metal objects. We discovered a few rockfaces with engravings and even some graves, but without mummies. The jungle is too humid for mummification.'

'Is it true that the excavation area is sealed off by the army?'

'Sealed off? That's not the right word. There are a few

soldiers up there to protect our personnel and keep out grave-robbers who could do a lot of damage.'

'So you have nothing to hide on the site? Theoretically, could tourists visit Buritaca 200 on organised tours?'

'We have nothing to hide, but we do not want tourists on the site. We are quite willing to allow access to experts, who could learn a lot from Buritaca 200. The social and ecological system of the complex is imposing. Although the Indian builders practised agriculture, traded with the sea ports and built cities, they did not destroy their environment.'

'Have you any objection to my visiting Buritaca 200?'

'Not the slightest!'

'How can I get there?'

'Only by helicopter. The flight from Bogotá to Santa Marta and back costs about 8,000 US dollars. But if you have the time and can wait for two months, because I have to give my university lectures, you can fly with me.'

A kind offer, but how to spend two months, a sixth of a year? I told myself that I must not be downhearted.

My first conversation with Soto Holguin was comparatively short, but later we had two lengthy talks at his flat in a high-rise building on Calle No. 7. Gradually I began to form a picture of the Lost City, as parts of the jigsaw fitted together. This is its story.

When the Spaniards Rodrigo de Bastidas and Juan de la Cosa were investigating the coasts of Venezuela in 1501, they also went in the direction of Panama. Obviously they must have traded with the Indians in the coastal regions, for they left one of their companions, Juan de Buenaventura, to learn the Indians' language. After all, merchants have to learn the language of their trading partners before they can cheat them.

The conquerors soon realised that Indians had gold objects to barter, as well as other things.

Professor Henning Bischof (2), the foremost expert on the Tairona culture, writes of the dense settlement in the region of the present-day port of Santa Marta:

In the sixteenth and early seventeenth centuries the Sierra Nevada looked quite different ... This conclusion is confirmed by the accounts of expeditions and battles, which show that the Spaniards had a much better range of vision than would have been the case in wooded mountain country. Basically, details of the density of the Indian population alone are enough to prove that the landscape must have changed considerably.

Rodrigo de Bastidas settled in Santo Domingo, the present-day capital of the Dominican Republic on the south coast of Haiti. In 1514 the Spanish king Carlos I appointed him Governor of the recently founded Province of Santa Marta. The Governor reached the small coastal town of Santa Marta with a body of two or three hundred men in June 1526.

During the next few decades the Spaniards were in almost continuous combat with the Tairona Indians, who defended themselves desperately against the white invaders who burnt their villages, plundered them and took the men prisoner or slaughtered them. The *conquistadores* knew that their barbaric methods had the blessing of the king in Madrid. He had issued a decree turning the Indians into slaves, outlawing them and allowing them to be killed or forced to perform the most degrading tasks.

The Indians met the Spaniards' modern weapons with stones, wooden clubs, spears and bows and arrows. Poisoned arrows. They got the poison from two natural sources, firstly the juice of the manzanilla tree, a highly poisonous type of spurge with fruit-like apples, which contained the poison. The arrows were dipped into the juice, dried in the air and wrapped in palm leaves so that the archers themselves would not be poisoned. Secondly, they tapped pacurine from the bark of the liana *Strychnos Toxifera*. In modern medicine it is known as curare, used as a nerve-relaxant. The Indians liked using pacurine because the game they killed remained edible in spite of the poison once the edges round the wound were cut out carefully.

Thousands of Spaniards died painfully by poisoned arrows in a hundred years' war against the Tairona, but the number of Indians who paid with their lives was far greater; it is estimated at 10,000.

Repelled by all the brutality, Juan de Castellanos (3), an eyewitness used to horrors, told how Captain Miguel Pinol gave orders that all Indians taken prisoner should have 'their noses, ears and lips cut off'. More then 70 Indian leaders were massacred, as well as women and children, and a severely wounded prince's son was executed, but not until the pagan son had been baptised into the Roman Catholic Church.

When it was all over the Spaniards had looted several hundred thousand gold pesos, as well as jewels and pearls. Indian settlements in the Sierra Nevada were destroyed. The few surviving Tairona hid in remote bays on the Caribbean coast.

The Tairona culture was wiped out and forgotten. Centuries passed. The jungle swallowed up the once flowering fields and settlements and cities. Save that in the region around Santa Marta it was rumoured that somewhere in the steaming forest-clad mountains there had once been an Indian tribe who saved a lot of gold from the Spaniards.

The kingdom of the Tairona had long since become the habitat of wild cats, apes, eagles and poisonous snakes. The humid flora of the primeval forest had conquered it. But gold has an irresistible fascination and men with gold-fever are not afraid of anything.

In autumn 1940 the treasure hunter and amateur archaeologist Florentino Sepúlveda met an old member of the Kogi Indian tribe in a quiet bay on the caribbean, only 20 km from Santa Marta. The old man told him that there were great cities and endless roads that had once been built by the Tairona in the immediate vicinity.

Sepúlveda, who was sixty years old himself, did not take the Indian's tales at their face value, but he found them interesting enough to tell his 19-year-old son Julio Cesar about them.

Julio Cesar, who did not know much more about the Spanish conquerors than that they loved gold, took the story seriously. For he was convinced of the existence of the legendary land of El Dorado and sensed that here was a chance to get rich quick — like winning the pools.

Julio Cesar followed the river Buritaca upstream from the coast. In the spring of 1975 he stumbled on one of the terraces of the Lost City. Convinced that he was on the right track, he took a spade and hacked a hole in the wall in front of him. After hours of laborious work he had to admit that the wall he was banging away at was part of a huge flight of steps.

This brought the gold-digger to his senses. He got on his horse and rode back to the port and seaside resort of Santa Marta, a difficult seven days' ride.

In a hotel bar, Julio Cesar did what a grave-robber should never do. He talked. Greedy for the gold, but not able to solve the problem of the site on his own, he showed the place in the jungle to some companions. Either out of envy or gold-fever, someone later shot Julio Cesar in the Lost City. Comrades dug his grave near the steps on which he had stumbled.

Then the grave-robbers, the *guaqueros*, swarmed in. They found their way into overgrown stone ruins. Soon Tairona cult artefacts appeared more and more frequently on the black market in antiques. The Colombian Institute for Anthropology and Archaeology got wind of this. When one grave-robber ransacked the site, the army took over the Lost City.

Archaeologists have been excavating in the jungle of the Sierra Nevada since 1976 and there is no end in sight yet, as Professor Soto told me. According to an assessment of the complexes so far excavated, 300,000 Indians must have lived there once. That is equal to the combined populations of Geneva and Berne.

Who were these wild Tairona Indians who managed to build these gigantic cities, who could not defend themselves against a handful of Spanish conquerors?

Soto told me that the present-day Kogi Indians on the coast and in the valleys of the Sierra Nevada are most probably direct descendants of the Tairona. His teacher, Professor Gerardo Reichel-Dolmatoff, spent years studying the life and history of the Kogi. In the process he established so many astonishing similarities between the present-day Kogi and the more ancient Tairona that we can assume that the Kogi descended from the Tairona.

Therefore groups of Tairona must have survived the Spanish massacres, preserved their ancient traditions and religious customs and handed them down to later generations. To find out who the Tairona were, I would have to concentrate on the Kogi, who are still living.

Once again Professor Preuss was the first man to take a scholarly interest in the Kogi and describe them in detail. After he had excavated parts of San Agustín from 1913 to

1914, he tackled the traditions of the Kágaba, as the Kogi were formerly called. Preuss discovered that the Kágaba-Kogi attributed the creation to the primordial mother Gauteóvan, who produced the sun and everything that existed from her menstrual blood. The four original priests who were the ancestors of the present-day Kogi priestly tribe also stemmed from Gauteóvan.

Tradition had it that the four original priests brought culture to the Indians, made laws and instructed them 'in all things'. The original priests had their home in space. Laws reached the Kágaba 'from outside'. It was said that these priests wore masks when they arrived and had their 'faces taken away'. If we assume that they had arrived on an interstellar flight, the faces would have been oxygen masks.

The priests bequeathed their office to their sons. They were brought up in the temple, serving a nine-year novitiate, so that the knowledge of the fathers was handed down untouched from one generation to another. The highest priests of the Kágaba-Kogi are called *Mama* (5). The *Mama* are more than what we normally understand by priests. The *Mama* is the absolute ruler of the tribe, whose orders must be followed blindly. There is no limit to the praise and punishment he can allot, because he knows that he is in direct succession to the original cosmic priests. Even today the *Mama* is convinced that he is in spiritual communication with the cosmos.

In order to reach this high-priestly rank, novices were shut up for nine years in total darkness and under close supervision in order to develop hypersensitive spirituality for cosmic contacts. The poor lads could not touch a woman during these nine years, do any work or eat salt. They were not served with food until midnight. It consisted of haricot beans, potatoes and snails; nothing with blood in it.

The primordial mother Gauteóvan and the four priests were not the only ones to emerge from the universe. There was also Uncle Nivaleue, who descended from heaven and made himself useful by laying out large fields. The demon Namsaui was another heavenly figure. The myths say that he was twice the size of normal men and killed men by the cold which flowed from him, leaving only their bones behind (4). It was said of Namsaui that his mask was red, his clothing blue and that he had protruding eyes over a very long nose. Namsaui was the lightning demon; he made the thunder and the snow that falls from heaven.

Professor Preuss described the Kágaba creation myth over 50 years ago. From the 30 pages he wrote I extract only the most important verses which show that their gods came from space and made man intelligent.

1st verse: The mother of our whole tribe bore us in the beginning. She is the mother of all kinds of men and she is the mother of all tribes ...

2nd verse: She alone is the mother of fire, the mother of the sun and the Milky Way ...

12th verse: And thus did the mother leave a memorial in every temple. Together with her sons Sintana, Seizankuan, Aluanuiko and Kultsavitabauya, she left behind songs and dances as memorials.

13th verse: That is what the priests, fathers and elder brothers reported.

Then come tales of the four priests fighting with demons and animals. 'Lightning bolts' are unleashed; there were flights all over the heavens and seeds of various plants were brought to earth. Masks of the gods were worn, one of them hidden in a mountain:

30th verse: Today it was set up to work on diseases and all kinds of evil and so that the novices who had learnt in the temple could talk to it. Afterwards the fathers, priests and elder brothers talked to it.

Did I read aright? Priests in ancient times are supposed to have talked to a mask to influence diseases? These descriptions only become intelligible when looked at from a modern point of view. The mask was a helmet with a built-in radio connection via which the priests received expert advice.

Knowledge of the Flood shows how far back the mythology of the Kágaba-Kogi reaches:

38th verse: Now centuries passed and then this world produced men with unnatural tendencies so that they used all kinds of animals to couple with. The mother desired the son, the father the daughter, the brother the sister, all being of the same blood.

39th verse: The prince Zantana saw this and opened the gates of heaven so that it rained for four years.

40th verse: When the priests observed that he would do this, the priest Seizankua built a magic ship and put all kinds of animals and other things inside it: the four-footed animals, the birds, and all kinds of plants did he place inside it. Thereupon the elder brother Mulkueikai entered the magic ship and closed the door.

41st verse: Then began red and blue rain which lasted for four years, and with the rain seas spread all over the world.

42nd verse: Meanwhile elder brother Mulkueikai lay in the magic ship which afterwards settled on the crest of the Sierra Negra. There he ventured out briefly and only very close to the ship. He stayed on the Sierra Negra for nine days.

43rd verse: After those nine days nine centuries passed before all the seas dried out, as the priests have handed down in our traditions.

44th verse: Now all evil people had perished, *and the priests, the elder brothers, all came down from heaven*. Whereupon Mulkueikai opened the door and placed all the birds and four-footed animals, all the trees and plants here on the earth. This did the divine person called father Kalgusiza bring about.

46th verse: And in all the temples they left behind a souvenir as a memorial.

How closely the texts resemble each other!

The Kágaba tradition mentioned sodomy, as did Moses in Genesis 19, before the destruction of Sodom and Gomorrah. The Sumerian *Epic of Gilgamesh* also includes a similar account of the Flood.

The Kágaba myth says that the priests all came down from heaven. The Sumerian King List says that: 'After the flood had receded, the kingdom came down from heaven again.' It sounds just like the Epic of Gilgamesh which relates that the 'gods' came down to earth after the great Flood.

Is there anyone barefaced enough to talk about coincidences when faced with such striking similarities? I mention only two myths identical with the Kágaba creation story, but they are found in ancient traditions all over the world. Everywhere real life experiences find their way into the myths.

Generations of priests continuously handed down the ancient knowledge of their cosmic teachers and preserved it. Professor Reichel-Dolmatoff (6) has shown that all the activities of the Kogi are still permeated by the cosmic laws of their Kágaba ancestors.

The Kogi are deeply religious. Their religious ideas are closely connected with their conception of order and happenings in the universe. Most villages have a chief who embodies governmental authority, but the real power of decision lies in the hands of the *Mama*, the native priests. These men have a thorough knowledge of tribal customs. They are not only shamans or medicine-men, but also in their priestly role take on tasks which they perform during ceremonial rituals after years of training.

During his years of study, Reichel-Dolmatoff discovered that all Kogi buildings could only by understood in the context of cosmic processes.

If a terrace, a house or a temple was to be built, the primary concerns were not only about the presence of water, light and shade, but the Kogi's cosmic relations to the constellations and the calendar were also 'built in'.

The Kogi looked on the cosmos as egg-shaped, demarcated by seven points: north, south, west, east, zenith, nadir (the lowest point of the heavens diametrically opposite to the zenith) and the centre. Within the space defined in this way lie nine layers, nine worlds, the middle or fifth layer representing our world. All the temples and ceremonial houses are models of the Kogi cosmos and follow this pattern.

Inside the ceremonial houses four divisions are superimposed. On the fifth division, the earth, the Kogi live, but symbolically four more divisions lead down into the earth, as symbol of the cosmos.

Apart from being religious centres, Kogi temples are also observatories. They are laid out in such a way that an accurate

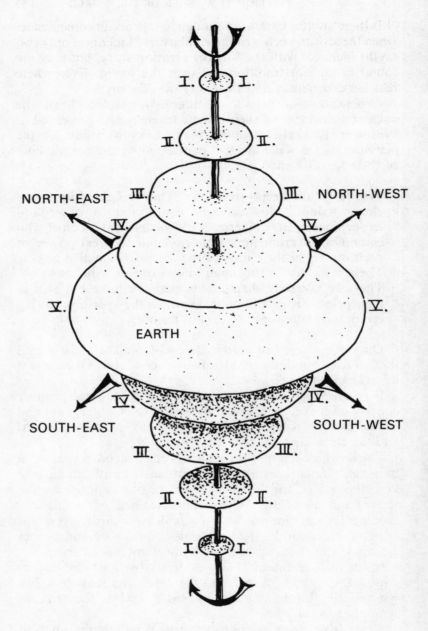

The Kogi looked on the cosmos as egg-shaped space.

calendar reading is possible at any time. Reichel-Dolmatoff (7) gives this example:

Men and women live apart. In every Kogi village there is a large round men's house on the roof of which a big post like a flagpole points up to heaven. Directly opposite — after all, the ladies must not be too far away — is the women's house, which is round, too. Two crossed beams emerge from the roof-ridge. Post and beams represent a symbolical act!

Precisely on 21 March, the beginning of spring, the post on the roof of the men's house throws a long shadow on the ground. It falls exactly between the shadows cast by the crossed beams on the women's house. The phallus penetrates the vagina, a symbol of spring. Seeds must be laid in the earth.

Inside the temple, a thick rope hangs from the ridge post through the four divisions down to the fifth, the earth. The high priest Mama is convinced that he is in direct contact with his cosmic teachers through this rope.

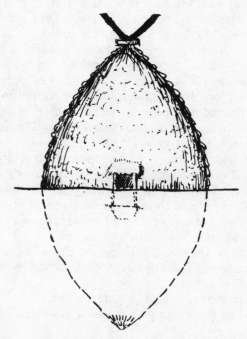

Cross-section of a Kogi house with its symbolic continuation into the ground.

What does this tell us? Nine years' confinement in the dark might develop telepathic abilities enabling men to make contact with extraterrestrials. We know that radio connections from star to star are too slow to make interstellar communication possible. Alpha Centauri, the nearest fixed star to the earth, is four light-years away, i.e. 4 times 9.46 times 10^{12} km. Questions from earth transmitted to Alpha Centauri by radio would not get a radio answer for eight years. But telepathy is as swift as thought and it is not bound by the physical laws of time and space. Could the Kogi's knowledge make the inaccessible intelligible to us?

When I had given my lectures in the Teatro Libertador and used up the time allotted for talking to Professor Soto and visits to libraries, I was burning to see the Lost City about whose builders I now knew quite a lot.

Salvation came from an angle indicated three months before, and then by a lucky chance.

I was invited as a guest to the Officers' Club of the FAC.* The air force owns a lovely clubhouse in the centre of Bogotá, an extensive one-storey building in a well-kept garden with a swimming pool. My invitation was for lunch.

From one o'clock onwards I sat on a dark-blue plush sofa next to Dr Forero, looking at photographs of famous Colombian aviators. Neither this nor an ice-cold vermouth had any effect on my stomach. It was rumbling irritably, craving nourishment. Colonel Baer-Ruiz, wearing a smart light-blue uniform, arrived about two o'clock. The first reasonable information about how I could get into the jungle near Santa Marta dried up in polite introductions to group captains and pensioned officers who kept on arriving in droves.

When we sat down at the beautifully set-out table around three o'clock, my stomach, as loud as a ventriloquist's voice, interrupted every conversation, while we chatted about God and the world and my books. I swore that I would get something out of them and after a few glasses of dry Chilean white wine I asked the company 'Gentlemen, how do I get to Buritaca 200?'

The officers looked at me in amazement.

'Where do you want to go?' asked a young pilot.

---

* *Fuerza Aerea Colombiana*, the Colombian Air Force.

The forest flora have forced their way through the man-made paving stones.

'The whole site has a plan, a gigantic plan...'

Above:
A last snapshot: Sylvia, Margarita, Hernando and the flight engineer, shortly before takeoff.

Overleaf
Left:
Millions of cubic metres of stone were shifted at Buritaca. How? The eighth wonder of the world?

Right:
We hastened up the main flight of steps to the landing terrace. The helicopter took off and the landing place was swallowed up in the maws of the greedy rain forest.

I soon realised that Buritaca 200 was so much double-Dutch to these aviators. Admittedly they had heard of the Lost City, but no one had even a rough idea where it was. Well briefed by Professor Soto, the little Swiss gentleman was able to give the astonished Colombians the exact geographical location of their national attraction.

I asked politely if there was any chance of looking for it in a helicopter. All the officers burst into a cascade of Spanish which I could no longer follow. Finally Colonel Baer told me that only the head of the air force, General Paredes Diago, could decide about my case. However he had just returned from a ten-day visit to the USA and his timetable was so booked up that he would not be able to receive me at once. *Mañana*.

'What a pity,' I said and saw my prey escaping. How was I to get into the jungle, unless I waited for two months and relied on Professor Soto?

Over coffee and brandy, I overheard someone saying that General Paredes Diago was interested in my books and was also a passionate pipe collector.

The pipe which opened up the jungle to me.

Pipe collector? An idea flashed through my brain.

Since I got hold of a patented model which makes tiresome cleaning with dirty fingers unnecessary, I smoke a pipe for lazy smokers while working or playing chess. This pipe does not have the classical curved bowl. A container closed by a filter holds the tobacco and is in a straight line with the mouthpiece. The container can easily be emptied into an ashtray by a slight pressure. I took a brand-new example out of my jacket pocket. 'Does the general know this sort of pipe?'

Colonel Baer was interested at once. I took the pipe to bits, put it together again and asked him to present it to the general with my compliments and possibly mention that he was the only man in Colombia who could help to solve my little problem.

Colonel Baer-Ruiz phoned me early the next morning to say that General Paredes Diago would expect me in the headquarters of the FAC at 4 p.m. Dr Forero also accompanied me on this vital visit.

The air force headquarters, a modern building of glass, steel and concrete, lies on the outskirts of Bogotá. My hand luggage was checked and our bodies were searched. After showing our own identity cards, a corporal pinned numbered cards to our chests, the only military identification I have ever worn.

On the way to the general's office past glass cases full of model aircraft of all periods, we civilians were given appraising looks by officers who were waiting for their appointments on leather settees. We only sat in the waiting room for a quarter of an hour and the door to the holy of holies opened.

General Paredes Diago, with five gold stars on his shoulder straps, held my pipe in his hand when he rose from behind his desk. He asked us to sit down in a corner while an orderly served coffee. My poor heart!

I gave the general a signed copy of the Spanish version of my book Signs of the Gods?, Profeta del Pasado. Warned in advance that the general was a busy man, I came straight to the point: I wanted a helicopter flight to Buritaca 200.

For a moment the general looked at me reflectively. Then he summoned his adjutant.

'What unit is stationed in Santa Marta?'

'The No. 5 Cordova Infantry Battalion, sir,' answered the young officer.

'Find out at once whether the battalion has a helicopter and whether the machine is ready for a special mission the day after tomorrow.'

A loudspeaker somewhere interrupted our conversation. The general spoke something in reply into his microphone. I could not understand a word. The general bowed to me and disappeared. Dr Forero gave the thumbs-up sign. We had won!

In a few minutes the general returned, handed me an envelope and wished me luck and success.

In the taxi I read what the general had dictated:

Fuerza Aerea Colombiana.
Senor Teniente Coronel.
Hector Lopez Ramirez Commandante Batallón de Infanteria No. 5 Cordova Santa Marta.
El señor Erich von Däniken está autorizado por este Comando para efectuar un vuelo en Helicótero Hughes que se encuentra en esa Unidad de la ciudad de Santa Marta a la ciudad perdida.
Cordial saludo.
General Raul Alberto Paredes Diago.
Commandante Fuerza Aérea.

[Lt Colonel Hector Lopez Ramirez
Officer commanding No. 5 Cordova Infantry Battalion Santa Marta
This order authorises Mr Erich von Däniken to fly from Santa Marta to the Lost City in the Hughes Helicopter belonging to your unit.]

The next day I landed in Santa Marta on the noon flight of Colombian Airways and lodged right by the sea in the Irotama, a hotel which had seen better days. I phoned repeatedly but I could not get in touch with Colonel Ramirez. At five o'clock in the afternoon it's packing-up time, as with soldiers all over the world. *Mañana.*

On Friday, 21 August, at 5.30 a.m., I was driven out to No. 5 Infantry Battalion. Two infantrymen with machine pistols searched me at the entrance before I could explain the reason for my visit, but the general's letter which I waved at them worked like an open sesame until a civilian in the colonel's

anteroom looked at it with wrinkled brows. Surprise depart-
ures from routine were unwelcome at such an early hour. The
civilian disappeared into the next door office without a word.

Although it was so early in the morning I was dripping
with sweat because of the high humidity. I sat on a wooden
bench, wiping the sweat from my forehead with a handkerchief
that was already wet, and waited. The civilian returned, sat at
his desk and said nothing. The waiting seemed endless. Was
there going to be some snag when I was almost there?

I determined to sit there quietly, but determined not to
budge until the general's order was carried out. *Basta.*

Basta!, repeated the young man in green uniform who was
leaning against the wall with his arms crossed. On the flap of
his right-hand breast pocket I saw the words Fuerza Aerea
Colombiana embroidered in silver. A pilot in the infantry?

He had to be my helicopter pilot! I spoke to him.

His name was Fernando, he said, and he was to fly a Mr
von Däniken to the Lost City, but he had not the faintest
idea where it was and the weather that day was not ideally
suited to the little Hughes. Besides the machine could only
stay airborne for two and a half hours. It could not spend
much time searching because if the city could not be found
in an hour and a quarter we should have to return.

Fernando did not see things through rose-coloured spec-
tacles. He gave a gloomy account of the difficulties he had
with the marijuana cultivators in the district. They were rightly
afraid of the military pilots and opened fire on them at random.
More than one aircraft had been shot down over the forests
and the crew had never been heard of again. Santa Marta
was a centre of the trade in marijuana, a city where life was
not worth twopence since trafficking in the drug had begun.
People could earn fantastic sums in a very short time and that
pushed up inflation. Morality went to pot and shoot-outs
were the order of the day. 'Santa Marta gold' was dealt with
on the international markets at top prices as being finest
quality marijuana.

Since the men stood to attention, the officer who looked
in and held the door open must be my Colonel Ramirez. I
leapt up, gave my name, received a brief searching look and
was invited to sit down in his office. Naturally we were served
coffee, of the kind that pours forth from morning to night.

Santa Marta — port and seaside resort on the Caribbean — is the centre of traffic in illegal 'Santa Marta gold', valuable marijuana.

Fernando described his difficulties. Colonel Ramirez interrupted him. 'Is there anyone in the battalion who knows the exact location of the Lost City?'

Ramirez gave an order over the loudspeaker, spread some military maps on the table and pointed with his finger. 'It's somewhere in that region.'

When I pointed out that it was on the River Buritaca, Fernando asked ironically if I knew the forest. He could not land there. I would either have to jump out or be let down on a rope ladder. I certainly had no desire to do that and said firmly, 'You can land in the forest on terraces that were built more than a thousand years ago!'

Professor Soto had told me that that was how he had reached the site.

'Do you believe that?' Colonel Ramirez looked at me sceptically.

'I know it for a fact.'

A corporal, who was undoubtedly of Indian blood, reported.

'You've been to the Lost City before?' asked Ramirez.

'Yes, Señor Comandante,' said the Indian, thumping his chest proudly.

'Then you shall go on the flight.'

Until that moment I did not realise that even Indians can turn white. The corporal crossed himself and his face, which had been radiant, turned ashen.

Together with Hernando, the Indian and a flight engineer, I clambered into the four-seater helicopter, which crossed Santa Marta with a deafening roar, then flew along the coast to the mouth of the Buritaca valley.

The natives were called Indians (Indios) by mistake. To the end of his days Columbus believed that the country he discovered was India and so named the inhabitants Indians. The Indian shouted something I did not understand and I saw that he was showing Hernando where to fly in sign language. Low cloud cover clung to the tops of the giant forest trees. Somewhere down below there were marijuana farmers, but I was more afraid of losing our way than their flintlocks. There was nothing to orientate oneself by. From above the green hell looked like an enormous greenish-black cauliflower. Dense and impenetrable.

The helicopter banked steeply and then I saw it: one terrace with a second and a third one below it Hernando had spotted it, too, and gave me a significant look. He landed the Hughes gently on the topmost terrace. He did not stop the rotor blades. They made a whirlwind in the still air. Hernando was anxious to take off again; he did not trust the weather.

'Back here in five hours,' I shouted and put up my hand with the fingers outspread. 'OK. In five hours,' he shouted back, pointing to the terrace on which we stood.

The helicopter rose up vertically; its clatter seemed to cling to trees and lianas. When the noise had faded, there was a moment's silence in the jungle, but the animals soon recovered from their fear of the noisy visit. Monkeys roared, birds chattered and invisible animals screamed. Wherever I went I was followed by buzzing mosquitoes which proved to be very attentive. I would gladly have walked around the jungle sauna

When the helicopter banked we saw a terrace suitable for landing in the dense jungle.

like Adam, but the repulsive biters made me realise in the most unpleasant way that I was not in Paradise. I read somewhere that there were about 1.5 million species of insects. The great majority of them were represented in Buritaca.

Now I was standing lost in the Lost city, probably the first European to do so. Certainly no European had as yet photographed or written about the site.

I like adventure, but I'm no hero. I am always getting into tricky situations against my will. I asked myself what would happen if the weather made landing impossible in five hours. Or supposing the only helicopter available crashed in the meantime.

What if Hernando was given a more important military mission? Spending the night here was not a very pleasant prospect, but what could I do about it? I shouldered my cameras and clambered down to the next terrace.

Opposite, on the cliff face, clung a wooden hut among tropical undergrowth, cedars, nut trees, eucalyptus trees, advocado pear trees, rubber trees, palms and ferns, all of them smothered in lianas. It had to be the archaeologists' camp. I shouted, but there was no answer. Heaven only knew where the team were digging today to keep the greedy jungle at bay from the ruins they had excavated. They must have seen and heard the helicopter.

Suddenly two soldiers appeared from nowhere. They were wearing jungle camouflage suits flecked with brown, green and red and were armed with rifles and pistols.

'*Buenos días, señores!*' I cried but got no reaction from their dark-brown faces. I still had two duty-free cigars in metal tubes bought on the Lufthansa flight and I gave them to the soldiers. They said, '*Gracias!*' and walked away. They were far from loquacious, but at least I knew that there were people somewhere in the green hothouse.

I slowly descended the endless steps which were a good 1.5 m wide and was surprised that the elliptical terrace on which we had landed was still within my field of vision. The lower I went, the more obvious it became that the topmost platform rested on a lower one, and that on another one and so on. A series of artificial stone plateaux carried the structure up to the summit.

Was I suffering from hallucinations? I met two delightful girls on a moss-covered path. One of them, wearing baggy trousers and a green safari blouse, smiled and shook me by the hand. 'My name is Sylvia. Welcome to Buritaca 200!'

The other Amazon, in blue jeans that showed off her appetising figure, a wide leather belt and a wide-brimmed straw hat, looked a little bit older than Sylvia. Margarita, the older girl, was an architect by profession; Sylvia, an archaeologist, had been working with the excavation team for more than half a year.

My Colombian forest angels asked me for a cigarette, the only thing they longed for at that moment. I gave them all I had left. These girls with their perfect English were just what I needed. They led me along stone paths through the tropical rain forest, commenting on the site as we went. The humidity remained steady, between 60 and 95 per cent.

Buritaca 200 lies to right and left of the little river that gave the town its name, clinging to the gorges of Cerro Corea, 3,055 m high. The structures are arranged in the form of terraces in several layers along a broad road. The main entrance to the town is 900 m high. From the end of a gorge, a steep flight of steps with a gradient of 50 degrees leads 1,100 m up to the large levelled terraces. The upper part seems to have been the centre of the city. An intricate mixture of 26 large and small terraces with areas varying between 50 and 880 sq. m occupy the heights. All these terraces have been excavated since 1976, a tremendous feat.

Complicated topographical conditions were laid down by nature. This means that the ancient architects had to level the mountain metre by metre to make room for the horizontal structures. They cut into the rock faces, filling in with stones, earth and supporting walls. The height of the wall varies from 60 cm to 10 m!

Integrated with walls and terraces, the excavators discovered a canalisation system which kept the vast complex dry in spite of the constant humidity and torrential rain.

Margarita explained to me that archaeologists divided Buritaca into four main sectors. In the first sector they found the remains of household objects such as stone mills for grinding corn, in the second pottery, such as scoops, vases and eating dishes, in the third, ceremonial artefacts including beautifully worked clay flutes, and in the fourth, cult objects such as priests' rings, figurines of the gods and funerary tributes.

In spite of these finds, archaeologists, especially Soto Holguin, the Director of Excavations, are faced with a problem. No one knows what Buritaca really was — a sanctuary on a vast scale, orientated to the firmament, the calendar? A priestly city inhabited solely by initiates in one vast monastery? A dormitory town in which 300,000 Indians slept before going to work somewhere else in the daytime? Was it a military outpost, a fortress?

However, scholars do agree that the builders of the jungle city included far-sighted architects and engineers with a variety of skills. The whole conception implies far-sightedness because the settlements in the Sierra Nevada cannot have been the work of one generation. The gigantic scale shows that there must have been an overall plan before the first great stones were moved. Astronomers must have been involved from the beginning, at least as advisers, as it has been proved that certain terraces are aligned on the constellations. The exemplary ecological system indicates the cooperation of engineers. There were only limited areas for cultivation, but maize, beans, manioc and potatoes to supply 300,000 Indians were cultivated without destroying the environment.

In order to understand the full significance of this achievement, one needs to know the state of affairs around Santa Marta before 1975, when the Sierra Nevada was placed under government protection. The population in the port, the smart seaside resort of Santa Marta, grew at an alarming rate. It overflowed the city limits and reached the slopes of the Sierra Nevada. The forest was burnt down. People planted coffee and bananas in the fertile soil for a couple of years and as yields decreased pushed further into the jungle, leaving behind the scars of civilisation. In this district, it rains virtually every day from April to November. Without the protective covering of the tropical trees and their network of roots in the ground, the soil is eroded. The land becomes arid and unfertile in a

The Tairona settled in the virgin forest, but they did not destroy it.

few years. Today the area around Santa Marta still bears tragic witness to the destructive type of agriculture practised by local settlers until 1975. A disaster.

All this happened in a relatively short time. Yet the Tairona lived in their cities for nearly a thousand years without destroying the virgin forest and still produced great quantities of agricultural products. How did the Tairona solve their ecological and agricultural problems? Professor Soto gave me this answer:

To achieve what was achieved at Buritaca there must have been a social organisation that differed from every other type. The Tairona Indians must have known and used something special. These people were anything but primitive and the modern world can only learn from them. We destroy tropical rain forests by slash and burn and keep on creating new environmental crises. The builders of these settlements proved that there are other ways of going about things.

At first I suspected that the topmost terrace had come about by a chance accumulation of stone slabs and blocks.

At first I suspected that the top terrace had been formed by a chance accumulation of stone slabs. I said as much to Sylvia and Margarita, but they pointed out that I was standing in a landscape intentionally laid out in a bizarre way, a landscape of stone circles, walls, ellipses, small towers, flights of steps and paths, in an indescribable confusion of shapes which would not have occurred to Pablo Picasso in his most daring period, when he was dissolving the objective into geometrical structures.

Sylvia pulled curtains of lianas aside and opened up a vista of new surprises which extended downhill to the River Buritaca and up to the rock faces. Wherever we went in this ill-understood monument to the past, we continuously came across artificially levelled surfaces. The Hanging Gardens of Semiramis in Babylon were looked on as the seventh wonder of the world. I make a plea for adding Buritaca as the eighth wonder of the world.

The girls watched me as I came on one surprise after another. My camera was clicking away constantly. If I could not prove

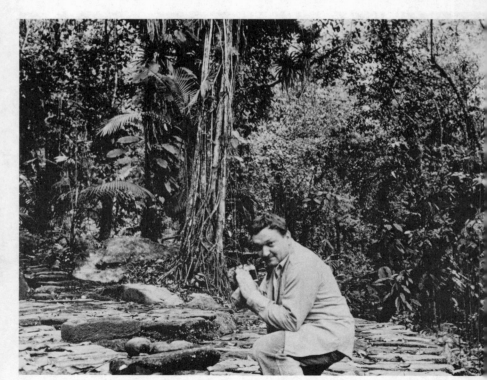

My camera never stopped clicking!

what I saw with photographs, no one would believe my description of the unique panorama. I had only to push aside the enormous leaf of a rubber tree to find myself staring at yet more massive accurately built walls and paths. With the explosive power of forest flora, thick corozo palms, bay-trees, cedars and ferns of every kind had forced their way through the neatly laid stones. It was a labyrinth as described in the dictionary: an arrangement of tortuous and deceptive paths from which it is difficult to find the way out. No matter whether I looked up, down, right or left, more platforms lay around me.

Mentally I conjured up the distant past when the priests worshipped their gods on the highest terraces, surrounded by thousands of Indians. When incense offerings rose to heaven from every platform and combined with the prayers, when the *Mama* were on intimate terms with the cosmos. If you block out in your imagination the trees which grow on the slopes today, a complete picture of this utopian landscape is present. Professor Soto's remark came into mind: 'The whole site has a plan, a gigantic plan, save that we do not know what it was for!'

One stone, more than two metres high, was covered with a plastic sack. I asked what it was. Sylvia and Margarita undid the rope and removed the protective covering from the monster, which was a monolith with many right-angled lines engraved on it. 'What is it?' I repeated.

Sylvia answered. 'The Indians say it was the plan of the complex.'

'A sort of city map, in other words?'

The girl nodded, but added at once that Professor Soto had his doubts about that. He had had the stone covered to save it from further weathering, in the hope that one day it would yield up its secret to scholars.

The literally indescribable noises of the forest were suddenly overpowered by the sound of water, although water was nowhere to be seen. Sylvia and Margarita were amused by my astonishment, then they pulled aside a curtain of lianas. A waterfall poured down the cliff until it was captured in a broad stone channel and led by another channel to a circular platform.

When you think that this area with its tropic rain was kept dry, your respect for the constructors increases enormously.

The Indians claim that this stone shows the town plan of Buritaca. It is not yet known if that is true.

I know the famous rice terraces in the mountains of the Philippines and the steep cultivated terraces of Machu Picchu in Peru. None of them is comparable with Buritaca 200.

The builders here did not set to work with monoliths of monstrous dimensions, as at Tiahuanaco and Puma Punku in Bolivia, or like Sacsayhuaman in Peru, and yet millions of cubic metres of stone were moved, for all the mountain slopes turn out to be artificially built on. After the first finds, the incredible astonishment began that always sets in in the presence of new discoveries. We shall keep on learning new things about Buritaca 200.

Suddenly monkeys and birds were silent. The noise of the helicopter's rotors echoed from the slopes. My five hours had actually passed.

Sylvia, Margarita and I hastened along narrow paths and across the main flight of steps to the landing terrace. Without the girls topographical knowledge, I would have been hopelessly lost.

Hernando was chatting to the soldiers who had been so taciturn with me. I pulled out of my pockets everything I did not need urgently and gave the conents to the helpful ladies: a light NASA windcheater, an anti-insect spray, plasters for cuts, a dynamo pocket torch, two screwdrivers and a measuring tape. Everything can be put to some use in the jungle.

The helicopter took off and flew low over the treetops in a curve back to the sea. Our landing place was left behind and was swallowed up by the mouth of the greedy rain forest.

Professor Soto had told me that the Kogi, like their ancestors the Tairona, looked on themselves as the 'elder brothers' of our planet. All foreigners are 'younger brothers' to them, for it was their ancient priests who brought life to their country from the cosmos.

The Tairona once had a blooming culture. Why do the Kogi dress so wretchedly today? Why have they stopped working in gold, spinning thread and weaving artistic materials? Why do they no longer paint mythical scenes on their ceramics?

The *Mama*, their high priests, the omniscient ones, tell the Kogi that it is no longer worth it. The gods had given the 'younger brothers' the opportunity to build dangerous playthings such as cannons, helicopters, car, submarines and rockets, but the 'younger brothers' did not know how to handle them. So the playthings would soon set the world on fire and there was no point in their former activities, although the *Mama*, and all the Kogi people are convinced that they are the ones who will preserve and continue the human race after the holocaust.

I am the opposite of a prophet of world disaster. I am an optimist, because I still rely on the intelligence of the men who recognise and try to eliminate the danger into which we have manoeuvred ourselves. Later I found that the mam-Kogi prophecies tally with the traditions of other Indian tribes from Chile to Canada.

In January 1980 there was an Indian Congress in Montreal attended by Indian priests from many territories. The representative of the Yanomano Indians from Venezuela told the Congress (8):

In the vicinity of the country where my people live there are some mountains which are sacred to us. We call one of them the 'bear', another the 'monkey' and a third the 'bird'. Long before the white men came, our medicine men visited these mountains many times. No one else was allowed to visit this district. These mountains conceal great powers and the ancient sages of our people speak of dangerous material that lies there. Our tradition says that if these mountains were destroyed, terrible misfortune would befall. Massive rainfall would flood everything and wipe out our people.

Then the Yanomano had something incredible to say. A few years ago Japanese scientists had drilled in the sacred mountains ... and they found uranium!

How could this knowledge (confirmed two years ago) have found its way into ancient Indian tradition a thousand years and more ago; who knew that certain mountains concealed dangerous materials? Who could predict that exploitation of the sacred mountains would unleash terrible misfortune?

As the primeval Indians were certainly incapable of producing measuring instruments to locate the uranium, we must ask: where did they get their knowledge? was their unspoilt religious sensitivity enough to localise the dangerous radiation? Or did they see creatures suffering an agonising death in the vicinity of their sacred mountains? That is quite possible, for nature does not look after her uranium as carefully as modern nuclear power stations treat uranium waste. Nature makes no distinction between the living and the dead.

Yet even if we admit that the Indians had sensed the presence of dangerous matter in their mountains in some way or other, their foreknowledge of the latent danger involved in exploitation is incomprehensible. We are proud of the fact that our high technology has made the invisible measurable. But who handed on the precognition?

Who told the Yanomano about the danger hidden in the mountains? The Indians themselves supply the answer. It was their heavenly teachers!

Of course it is easy enough to dismiss the 'heavenly teachers' as figments of the imagination dreamed up by the primeval Indians, but that leads us into a complete cul-de-sac. Then we are implying that the narrators of all Indian tribes, and *mutatis mutandis* our biblical prophets, cheated and lied in their accounts of conversations with the heavenly ones.

A prophet like the biblical Enoch did not say that he had spoken to visions or travelled in the realms of fancy. Enoch makes it quite clear that he spoke to teachers who came from heaven and that they instructed him in his activities. So were Enoch, Moses, Gilgamesh, the Yanomano and Hopi Indians, the Dogon Negroes in Central Africa, the ancient Indian sages and the Kogi all lying? Are we dealing with a world-wide Mafia of imaginative storytellers?

The second 'solution' of misunderstood mythological messages and stone witnesses from the remote past by psychological interpretations founders on the hard facts which do not tolerate lengthy attempts to lay verbal smokescreens. Buritaca 200 exists. The cosmological model stems from an as yet unverifiable past. It had been in existence long before the white man occupied the terrain centuries ago and 'discovered' the Indians. They would have existed and continued to exist even if the white men had not scared them away and ill-treated them.

The way may be unpleasant and barely accessible to our scientists, but it is the only one that leads to the goal. The primordial teachers were extraterrestrials.

If we accept this (to me banal) fact, the whole history of

mankind would be brilliantly illuminated. It is high time to pull this wisdom tooth. It is high time to investigate the claims of the Kogi that their ancient priests had left in the temples 'memories' which more advanced men would understand. Perhaps the stone phalluses that rear up to heaven are symbols of the life that came 'from above'. Perhaps the 'genetic disc' is a pointer to the origin of the first life. Perhaps the engravings on the Tunja stones contain formulas giving information about the sojourn of the extraterrestrials. Perhaps the Archaeological Park at San Agustín is a gigantic memorial that was left behind – as a memory of the future.

Our blue planet affords an overpowering number of memories. What must happen before science finally takes notice of them? It will be too late after a global catastrophe. We can no longer afford to overlook warnings or ignore possible remedies.

We are not only responsible for what we do, but also for what we leave undone!   (Molière, 1622–73)

Picture Acknowledgements

The pictures on pages 2 to 7 were kindly put at my disposal by the Church of Jesus Christ of Latter-day Saints, Salt Lake City (USA)

Josef Blumrich: Page No. 19 (from *The Spaceships of Ezekiel*, Bantam Books, 1974)

Manfred Steinlechner: Indian ink drawings on pages 42, 50, 51, 61, 66, 142

Professor Jaime Gutierrez, Bogotá: Page Nos. 145–148

Patrick Utermann: Sketches page Nos. 184 and 185

Willi Dünnenberger: Page No. 187

All other illustrations are by the author

Bibliography

1   Legendary Times!

1. *The Book of Mormon*, 16th edn, 1966
2. HINCKLEY, Gordon B., *The Truth Re-established. Brief sketch of the History of the Church of Jesus Christ of Latter-day Saints*, 1978
3. BIN GORION, Micha Josef, *Die Sagen der Juden von der Urzeit*, Frankfurt, 1919
4. BURROWS, Millar, *More Light on the Dead Sea Scrolls*, London, 1958
5. WUTTKE, Gottfried, *Melchisedech, der Preisterkönig von Salem, Eine Studie zur Geschichte der Exegese*, Giessen, 1929
6. BONWETSCH, Nathanael G., *Die Bücher der Geheimnisse Henochs, Das sogenannte slawische Henochbuch*, Leipzig, 1927
7. *Die Heilige Schrift des Alten und des Neuen Testaments*, Stuttgart, 1972
8. HERTZBERG, H. W., 'The Melschisedek Traditions', *The Journal of the Palestine Oriental Society*, Vol. VIII, Jerusalem, 1928
9. LAMBERT, Wilfried G. and MILLARD, Alan Ralph, *Atrahasis, The Babylonian Story of the Flood*, Oxford, 1970
10. SITCHIN, Zecharia, *Der Zwölfte Planet*, Unterägeri bei Zug, 1979
11. BLUMRICH, Josef F., *The Spaceships of Ezekiel*, Bantam Books, 1974
12. HEYERDAHL, Thor, *Early Man and the Ocean*, Allen & Unwin, 1978
13. MADER, A. E., 'New Dolmen Finds in West Palestine', *The Journal of the Palestine Oriental Society*, Vol. VII, Jerusalem, 1927
14. BÄRWOLF, Adalbert, 'Radar entschleiert die Äcker de Maya', *Die Welt*, Hamburg, 6 September 1980

15. CORDAN, Wolfgang, *Das Buch des Rates Popol Vuh — Schöpfungsmythos und Wanderung der Quiché-Maya*, Düsseldorf, 1962
16. HASSLER, Gerd von, *Noahs Weg zum Amazonas*, Hamburg, 1976
17. HONORÉ, Pierre, *Ich fand den Weissen Gott*, Frankfurt, 1965
18. HAMMOND, Norman, 'The Earliest Maya', *Scientific American*, New York, March 1977
19. TALMAGE, James E., *The articles of faith. An Examination and Consideration of the Main Doctrines of the Church of Jesus Christ of Latter-day Saints*, Salt Lake City, undated
20. MAZAR, Benjamin, *Der Berg des Herrn — Neue Ausgrabungen in Jerusalem*, Bergisch Gladbach, 1979

2   In the Beginning Everything Was Different

1. MAZAR, Benjamin, *Der Berg des Herrn — Neue Ausgrabungen in Jerusalem*, Bergisch Gladbach, 1979
2. TELLO, Julio C., 'Discovery of the Chavín Culture in Peru', *American Antiquity*, Vol. IX, No. 1, Menasha, 1943
3. STINGL, Miloslav, *Die Inkas — Ahnen der 'Sonnensohne'*, Düsseldorf, 1978
4. KAUFFMAN DOIG, Federico, 'La cultura Chavín', *Las Grandes Civilizaciones del Antiguo Peru*, Tomo III, Lima, 1963
5. NACHTIGALL, Horst, *Die amerikanischen Megalithkulturen*, Berlin, 1958
6. DISSELHOFF, H. D., *Das Imperium der Inka*, Berlin, 1972
7. PÖRTNER, Rudolf and DAVIES, Nigel, *Alte Kulturen der Neuen Welt, Neue Erkenntnisse der Archäologie*, Düsseldorf, 1980
8. TRIMBORN, Hermann, *Das Alte Amerika*, Stuttgart, 1959
9. HUBER, Siegfried, *Im Reich der Inka*, Olten, 1976
10. KATZ, Friedrich, *The Ancient American Civilisations*, Weidenfeld & Nicolson, 1969
11. FRANZ, Heinrich G., 'Tiermaske und Mensch-Tier-

Verwandlung als Grundmotive der altamerikanischen Kunst', *Jahrbuch des Kunsthistorischen Instituts der Universität Graz*, 1975

12. WEDEMEYER, Inge von, *Sonnengott und Sonnenmenschen*, Tübingen, 1970

13. KRICKEBERG, Walter, *Altmexikanischen Kulturen*, Berlin, 1975

14. DISSELHOFF, H. D., *Alt-Amerika*, Baden-Baden, 1961

15. SÉJOURNÉ, Laurette, *Altamerikanische Kulturen*, Vol. 21, Frankfurt, 1971

16. WILLEY, Gordon R., 'The Early Great Styles and the Rise of the Pre-Columbian Civilisations', *American Anthroplogist*, Vol. 64. 1962

17. LOTHROP, Samuel K., *Essays in Pre-Columbian Art and Archaeology*, Harvard University Press, Cambridge, Mass., 1964

18. BENNETT, Wendell C., 'The North Highlands of Peru, Part 2, Excavations at Chavín de Huantar', *Anthropological Papers of the American Museum of Natural History*, Vol. 39, New York, 1944

19. EISSFELDT, Otto, *Einleitung in das Alte Testament*, Tübingen, 1964

20. BURCKHARDT, Georg, *Gilgamesh — Eine Erzählung aus dem alten Orient*, Insel Verlag, undated

21. WILLEY, Gordon R., 'The Chavín Problem', *Southwestern Journal of Anthropology*, Vol. 7, No. 2, Albuquerque, 1951

22. DAVIES, Nigel, *Voyagers to the New World — Fact or Fantasy*, Macmillan, 1979

23. BURLEIGH, Richard, 'Scientific Methods of Dating', *Cambridge Encyclopedia of Archaeology*, Cambridge University Press, 1980

24. COE, Michael D., 'Olmec and Chavín: Rejoinder to Lanning', *American Antiquity*, Vol. 29, No. 1, Salt Lake City, 1963

25. KANO, Chiaki, 'The origins of the Chavín culture', *Studies in Pre-Columbian Art and Archaeology*, No. 22, Washington, 1979

26. KUBLER, George, *The Art and Architecture of Ancient America*, Harmondsworth, 1979

27. BLUMRICH, Josef F., *Kasskara und die Sieben Welten*, Düsseldorf, 1979

General
MÖLLER, Gerd and Elfride, *Peru*, Pforzheim, 1976
MASON, Alden J., *The Ancient Cities of Peru*, Pelican, Edinburgh, 1957
MIDDENDORF, E. W., *Das Hochland von Peru*, Vol. III, Berlin, 1895
KRICKEBERG, Walter, *Pre-Columbian American Religions*, Weidenfeld & Nicolson, 1961
WAISBARD, Simone, *Die Kultur der Inkas*, Zurich, 1980
RAIMONDI, Antonio, *El Peru*, Vol. I, Lima, 1940

3   A Case for Heinrich Schliemann
 1. BLUMRICH, Josef F., *The Spaceships of Ezekiel*, Bantam Books, 1974
 2. LAING, Bernhard, *Ezechiel — Der Prophet und das Buch*, Darmstadt, 1981
 3. KAUTZSCH, Emil, *Die Apokryphen und Pseudepigraphen des Alten Testaments*, Vol. II, Ch. 7, Das Leben Adams und Evas, Hildesheim, 1962
 4. GRÜNWEDEL, Albert, *Mythologie des Buddhismus in Tibet und in der Mongolei*, Leipzig, 1900
 5. BOPP, Franz, *Ardschuna's Reise zu Indra's Himmel*, Berlin, 1824
 6. LINDBLOM, J., *Prophecy in Ancient Israel*, Oxford, 1962
 7. KEEL, Othmar, *Zurück von den Sternen*, Fribourg, 1970
 8. BEYERLEIN, W., *Herkunft und Geschichte der ältesten Sinai-Traditionen*, 1961
 9. DUMMERMUTH, Fritz, Separatdruck der theologischen Fakultät der Universität Basel, *Theol. Zeitschrift*, No. 17, 1961 and No. 19, 1963
10. DUMMERMUTH, Fritz, 'Biblische Offenbarungsphänomene', *Theologische Zeitschrift*, No. 21, 1965
11. TORREY, C., *Pseudo-Ezekiel and the Original Prophecy*, New Haven, 1930
12. SMEND, Rudolf, *Der Prophet Ezechiel*, Leipzig, 1880

13. BAUMGARTNER, W., *Hebraisches Schulbuch*, 26th edn, Basle, 1971
14. EICHRODT, W., *Das Alte Testament deutsch — Der Prophet Hesekiel*, Göttingen, 1968
15. PRAGER, Mirjam and STEMBERGER, Günter, *Die Bibel*, Salzburg, 1976
16. RICHTER, G., 'Der ezechielsche Tempel — Eine exegetische Studie über Ezechiel', *Beiträge zur Förderung christlicher Theologie*, 16. Jahrgang, Heft 12, Tübingen, 1912
17. REUSS, Eduard D., *Das Alte Testament — die Propheten*, Vol. 2, Braunschweig, 1892
18. HAUCK, Albert D., *Realencyklopädie für Protestantische Theologie und Kirche*, Chap. Ezekiel, Graz, 1969
19. CHIPIEZ, Charles and PERROT, Georges, *Le temple de Jérusalem et la maison du Bois-Liban, Restitués d'après Ezéchiel et le livre des Rois*, Paris, 1889
20. THENIUS, Otto, *Die Bücher der Könige — Kurzgefasstes exegetisches Handbuch zum Alten Testament*, Leipzig, 1849

General
BRUGG, Elmar, *Tragik und schöpferischer Mensch*, Baden/ Switzerland, 1965
ZIMMERLI, Walther, *Ezechiel*, Vol. XIII/2, Neukirchen-Vluyn, 1969
BAUMANN, Eberhard D., 'Die Hauptvisionen Hesekiels', *Zeitschrift für die Alttestamentliche Wissenschaft*, Vol. 67, Berlin, 1956

4 The Strategy of the Gods

1. 'Indio-Kultur im Dschungel, *Der Spiegel*, 1 February 1981
2. STÖPEL, Theodor K., *Südamerikanische prähistorische Tempel und Gottheiten*, Frankfurt, 1912
3. PREUSS, Theodor K., *Monumentale vorgeschichliche Kunst*, Göttingen, 1929
4. NACHTIGALL, Horst, *Die Amerikanischen Megalithkulturen*, Berlin, 1958

5. SOTO, Alvaro, *San Agustín*, Instituto Colombiano de Antropología, Bogotá, undated
6. DISSELHOFF, H. D., 'Die Kunst der Andenländer', *Alt-Amerika — Die Hochkulturen der Alten Welt*, Baden-Baden, 1961
7. KAPP, Martin, 'Im finstern zwanzigsten Jahrhundert', *Information der Internationalen Treuhand AG*, Heft 64, 1981
8. NIEL, Fernand, *Auf den Spuren der Grossen Steine*, Munich, 1977
9. HITZ, Hans-Rudolf, *Als man noch Protokeltisch sprach, Versuch einer Entzifferung der Inschriften von Glozel*, Ettingen, 1982
10. THÜRKAUF, Max, *König Nobels Hofstaat*, Schaffhausen, 1981
11. PRIANA, Miguel, *El jeroglifico Chibcha*, Bogotá, 1924
12. RUZO, Daniel, *La historia fantastica de un descubrimiento*, Mexico City, 1974
13. 'Stinkbomben in Atomlagern', *Der Spiegel*, 1981/51
14. SIMON, Pedro, *Noticias historiales de las conquistas de tierra en las Indias occidentales*, Bogotá, 1882–90
15. NACHTINGALL, Horst, *Alt-Kolombien*, Berlin, 1961
16. PAUWELS, Louis and BERGIER, Jacques, *Aufbruch ins dritte Jahrtausend*, Bern, 1962

General

BRAY, Warwick, *El Dorado*, New York, 1974
BUCHANAN, D., 'A Preliminary Decipherment of the Glozel Inscriptions', *The Epigraphic Society*, Vol. IX, No. 226, San Diego, Ca., 1981
CRICK, Francis, *Life Itself, Its Origin and Nature*, London, 1981
CHAVES, Eduardo B., *Mensagem dos Deuses*, Lisbon, 1977
FRADIN, Emile, *Glozel et ma vie*, Paris, 1979
HORNICKEL, Ernst, *Sonne, Strand und sowieso — Von Inseln, Küsten und lockenden Wassern*, Stuttgart, 1975
HOYLE, Fred, *Diseases from Space*, London, 1979
HOYLE, Fred and WICKRAMASINGHE, N. C., *Evolution from Space*, London, 1981
POSADA OCHOA, Mario, *Gold Museum*, Bank of the Republic, Bogotá, 1968

5   The Eighth Wonder of the World

1. SOTO, Alvaro, *Buritaca 200* (Ciudad Peridida), Bogotá, undated.
2. BISCHOF, Henning, *Die spanisch-indianische Auseinandersetzung in der nördlichen Sierra Nevada de Santa Marta (1501–1600)*, Bonn, 1971
3. CASTELLANOS, Juan de, *Elegias de varones ilustres de Indias*, Madrid, 1914
4. PREUSS, Theodor Konrad, *Forschungsreise zu den Kágaba*, Vienna, 1926
5. KRICKEBERG, Walter and TRIMBORN, Hermann (and others), *Pre-Columbian American Religions*, Weidenfeld & Nicolson, 1961
6. REICHEL-DOLMATOFF, Gerardo, 'Die Kogi in Kolombien', *Bild der Völker*, Vol. 5, Wiesbaden, undated
7. REICHEL-DOLMATOFF, Gerardo, 'Templos Kogi — Introduccion al simbolismo y a la astronomía del espacio sagrado', *Revista Colombiana de Antropologia*, Vol. XIX, Bogotá, 1975
8. 'Indianer prophezeien den Untergang des Weissen Mannes', *Weser-Kurier*, 21 January 1980

General
REICHEL-DOLMATOFF, Gerardo and Alicia, *The people of Aritama*, London, 1961
REICHEL-DOLMATOFF, Gerardo, *Colombia — Ancient Peoples and Places*, London, 1965
SOTO, Alvaro and CADAVID, Gilberto, 'Buritaca 200', *Revista Lampara*, Bogotá, No. 76, Vol. XVII, December 1979

Index

Aaron 12
Abraham 12, 15, 64
Adam 11, 13, 29, 64
Agamemnon 76
Ajiaco (national dish) 133
Aldebaran 11
Alexandria 11
Alto de los Idolos v. San Agustín, Hill
    of the Idols
Alto de las Piedras v. San Agustín, Hill
    of the Foot Washing
Alto de las Piedras v. San Agustín, Hill
    of the Stones
Aluañuiko 181
Amazon 97, 108, 119
    basin 97, 108
Apis 65
Ardjuna 84
Ark (Noah's) 9
Atlantic 9, 97, 108
Atrahasis 16, 17
Avebury 135
Aztecs 11, 21, 25, 126

Babel, Tower of 8, 10, 13, 16
Babylon 33, 100, 141, 144, 198
Baer-Ruiz, Col. 130–1, 155, 171, 173,
    186–7
Barradas, Perez de 117
Barreto, Felicitas 106
Bastidas, Rodrigo de 176–7
Bat Enosh 13, 15
Bennett, Wendell C. 61–2
Bergier, Jacques 166
Beyerlin, W. 84
Bischof, Henning 36, 176
Blumrich, Josef F. 18–19, 70, 80–1, 119
Book of Enoch 12
Book of Ether 8, 16–17, 32
Book of Ezekiel 18–19, 77–84, 85–6, 89,
    90, 96, 99
Book of Kings 93
Book of Mormon 5, 7, 8, 16, 27, 29, 32,
    33, 71, 100
Book of Nephi 8, 27–9, 30, 32, 33, 71, 72
Brittany 107, 125, 135–6
Buenaventura, Juan de 176
Buritaca (River) 175, 178, 192, 194, 198
Buritaca 173, 175–6, 178, 186, 188,
    194–201

Burleigh, Richard 68

Calendar 20, 135
Calima Indians 34, 167–8
Caqueta (River) 108
Caribbean Sea 104, 175, 177
Caribes Indians 161–2
Carnac 112
Carthago 8
Castellanos, Juan de 177
Cerro Corea 194
Charles I (of Spain) 177
Chavín de Huantar 32, 33, 35, 63, 65,
    68–9, 71–4, 96–100
    Culture 45, 57–8, 63–4, 68
    El Castillo 36–40, 45, 58, 72, 97, 98
    El Lanzon 41–4, 59
    Style 58–62, 65, 68
Chebar (River) 77, 83, 100
Cherubs 49, 89
Chibcha Indians 155, 161, 175
Chicha (drink) 132
Chiminigagua (God) 161–2
Chipiez, Charles 93
Chumbaba 63
Church of Jesus Christ of Latter-day
    Saints 5–7, 29, 32
Ciudad Perdida v. Lost City
Codazzi, General 105
Columbus, Christopher 192
Compass 28–9, 100, 135
Cordan, Wolfgang 29
Cordova 189
Cortez, Hernando 24
Cosa, Juan de la 176
Cowdery, Oliver 6
Cromlech 135–6, 138
Crucuno 135–6
Cubit 93, 97
Cumorah (Hill of) 3, 4
Curare 177
Cylinder seals 59

Darwin, Charles Robert 152, 154
Davies, Nigel 54, 64
Diago, Paredes 187–9
Disselhoff, H. D. 54, 58, 117
Divinities, Winged 59
Dogon negroes 203
Dolmen 107, 112–13, 125
Dummermuth, Fritz 84

Dupaix (Researcher) 112

Eden, Garden of 14
Eichrodt, Walther 98
Einstein, Albert 15
El Castillo v. Chavín de Huantar
El doble yo v. San Agustín Double I
El Dorado 162–3
El Fuerte 117–18
El Lanzon v. Chavín de Huantar
Elijah (Prophet) 62, 84
Enki (God) 16–17
Enkidu 63
Enoch (Prophet) 12–13, 16, 29, 62, 84, 203
Enuma Elīs 16–17
Esqualanta, Carlos 131
Eve 64, 84, 90
Evolution, Theory of 152–5
Ezekiel (Prophet) 27, 33, 35, 74, 77–84, 85–100
    see also Book of Ezekiel

Facatativá 157, 158–9, 160–2, 168
Forero, Juan Carlos 104, 131, 134, 136, 155, 162–3, 164, 165
Forero, Miguel 102–4, 130, 131, 134, 155, 165, 171, 172–3, 186, 188–9
Fradin, Emile 141
Franz, H. G. 55
Freud, Sigmund 123
Friedell, Egon 75

Gallego, Jairo 131–3, 136
Gauteóvan (primordial mother) 180
Genetic disc 138–9, 144–51, 155, 204
Gilgamesh 63, 203
    Epic of 16, 17, 63, 182
Glozel 141–2
Goethe, Johann Wolfgang von 131
Gold Museum, Bogotá 164–71
Guatavita (Lake of) 163–4
Guayaba (fruit) 133
Gutierrez, Jaime 139–41, 142–51, 155, 157, 159

Hammond, Norman 25
Hanging Gardens 198
Harris, Martin 6
Hassler, Gerd von 24
Hector 76
Herod (King) 37
Heyerdahl, Thor 20, 24
Hissarlik 76, 98
Hitz, Hans-Rudolf 141
Homer 75–6, 82, 93
Hopi Indians 149, 203
Hospedería Duruelo 133
Hoyle, Fred 151–3, 155
Huber, Siegfried 55, 65
Huycaybamba 97

Inca 21, 25, 34, 144, 175
Israeli Museum, Jerusalem 99

Japurá (River) 108, 119
Jared 8, 16
Jaredites 8, 9, 10, 16, 17, 27, 29
Jefferson, Thomas 158
Jerusalem 11, 14, 27, 30, 32, 33, 36, 37–8, 58, 72, 74, 86, 91, 94–5
Job 62–3
Judah, King of v. Zedekia

Kágaba Indians 16, 21, 180–6
Kalgusiza 182
Kashiri (drink) 132
Katz, Friedrich 55, 64
Keel, Othmar 84
King Nobel's State 127, 151, 166
Knapp, Martin 129
Kogi Indians 178, 179–86, 201–4
Krickeberg, Walter 57
Kukulkan (God) 162
Kultsavitabauya 181

La Paz 133
La Soledad 112
La Venta 68
Lamech 13–14, 15
Lao-tse 125
Lattion, Raphy 138, 140, 147–8, 151
Lehi 27–8
Lessing, Gotthold Ephraim 32
Leyva 131, 138
    Stones 134–7
Lima 35
Lincoln, Abraham 158
Lindblom, J. 84
Longe (River) 159
Lost City 173, 175–6, 178, 186, 190–201
    see also Buritaca
Louquo 162

Machu Picchu 175, 201
Madeira (River) 119
Magdalena (River) 105, 107, 108, 124, 127
Mahabharata 84
Mama (Priests) 180, 183, 185, 199, 201–2
Mamore (River) 119
Manáus 119
Manioc 162
Marañon (River) 97–8
Marcahuasi 158
Masma Culture 157
Maya 11, 21, 22, 25, 141
Melchizedek 14–16, 17, 26, 29
Menhirs 112–13, 125, 135–6
Michael (Archangel) 14, 15
Moctezuma 24, 132
Mojós Indians 64
Monte Albán 68
Montesquieu, Charles de 160–1

Montreal 202
Moore, Henry 125
Moque (incense) 163
Morlet, Antonin 141
Mormons 8, 28, 30
Moroni (divine messenger) 2–3, 5, 8
Moses 12, 14, 22–3, 64, 72, 182, 203
Mosna (River) 37, 39, 63, 97
Mount Rushmore 158
Muisca Indians 161–3, 164
Mulkueikai 16, 182
Museo Antropológico y Arqueológico, Lima 49
Museo Nacional de Antropologia, Mexico City 68
Museo del Oro v. Gold Museum
Mycenae 76

Nachtigall, Horst 55, 110, 117
Namsaui (Demon) 180–1
Napoleon 1
Nazca 21, 36
    Period 133
Nephi 27–8, 29, 30, 33, 71–2
Nephites 29, 30, 71, 100
Niel, Fernand 135
Nimrod (Valley) 8
Nir 14
Nivaleue 180
Noah 12, 13–14, 15–16, 17–18, 21, 26, 29, 64
Nuclear reactor 18

Oaxaca 112
Oberem, Udo 36
Oberth, Hermann 36, 151
Olmecs 57, 68–70
Orion 11
Orteguaza (River) 108

Pacific 108
Pacurine poison 177
Padmasambhava 84
Page, Hiram 6
Palmyra (New York State) 1, 3
Palpa 20
Parque Arqueológico de Facatativá 157, 159, 160–2
Patia (River) 108
Pauwels, Louis 166
Pedro, Simon 161
Pérez de Quesada, Hernán 163
Pergamon 10
Perrot, Georges 93
Philip II (of Spain) 164
Piedras de Leyva v. Leyva Stones
Peidras de Tunja v. Tunja Stones
Piñol, Miguel 177–8
Piripiri 159
Pitalito 104
Pizarro, Francisco 133

Popol Vuh 22–3, 24, 27, 29
Pörtner, Rudolf 54
Presbyterians 1
Preuss, Konrad Theodor 106–7, 126, 179–81
Priam 76
Priana, Miguel 155
Puma Punku 201
Purace 108
Pyramids 22

Quebrada de Lavapatas v. San Agustín, Spring of the Foot Washing
Quetzalcóatl (God) 24
Quiché Maya 22, 27, 29
Quimbaya Indians 167
Qumran 13, 99

Raimondi, Antonio 54
    Stele 52–7, 59
Ram jet drive 18
Ramirez, Hector Lopez 189–92
Raziel (Angel) 11, 12, 16
Reichel-Dolmatoff, Gerardo 179, 183–5
Reuss, Eduard 94–5
Rincon, Bernardo 142
Rollright 135
Roosevelt, Theodore 158
Russell, Bertrand 172
Ruzo, Daniel 157–8

Sacsayhuaman 20, 201
Salem, King of, v. Melchizedek
Salt Lake City 5
San Agustín 104–29, 179, 204
    Culture 105
    Double I 120–1, 125, 126
    El Tablon 107
    Forest of the Statues 107, 108–12
    Hill of the Foot Washing 107, 120–3
    Hill of the Idols 107, 124
    Hill of the Stones 125–6
    La Chaquira 107, 127
    Spring of the Foot Washing 107, 114–20
Santa, Juan de 105
Santa Marta 104, 171, 173, 174, 176–8, 186, 188–92, 196
    'gold' 190
Sapphire 11, 12, 29
Sariah 27–8
Schliemann, Heinrich 74, 75–6, 81, 93, 98
Schopenhauer, Arthur 57
Sebeok, Thomas 160
Second face 126
Seizankua 182
Seizankuan 181
Selye, Hans 77, 101
Semiramis 198
Sepúlveda, Antonio de 164
Sepúlveda, Florentino 178

Sepúlveda, Julio César 178–9
Sete Cidades 149, 159
Shaw, Bernard 80
Shrine of the Book 99–100
Sierra Negra 182
Sierra Nevada 104, 173, 175, 176, 178, 179, 195–6
Sinai (Mount) 73
Sintana 181
Sirius 11
Sitchin, Zecharia 16
Sitting Bull 158
Smend, Rudolf 85, 93–4
Smith, Hyrum 6, 8
Smith, Joseph 1–8, 12, 16, 17, 27, 29
Smith, Joseph sen. 3, 6
Smith, Samuel H. 6
Solomon 12, 73
    Temple 29, 31, 32, 33, 35–8, 58, 71, 72–3, 86, 91, 94, 95, 96, 98, 100
Sopranima 14, 15
Soto Holguin, Alvaro 102, 104, 130, 131, 151, 165, 173–6, 179, 186–7, 191, 195, 197, 199, 201
South Dakota 158
Stegosaurus 157
Stingl, Miloslav 41, 44, 54, 58
Stonehenge 112, 135
Stöpel, Karl Theodor 105
Strychnos toxifera 177
Stübel, Alphons 105
Sumerian King Lists 182
Sutatausa 142

Tairo 175
Tairona Indians 175, 177–8, 179, 197, 201
    Culture 175, 176, 178, 179, 201
Talmage, James E. 29
Tapi 21
Tello, Julio C. 39, 59, 64
    Obelisk 49–51, 59
Tenochtitlán 24

Thenius, Otto 94
Thummim (oracle stones) 3, 5, 6
Thürkauf, Max 151
Tiahuanaco 20, 201
Titus Flavius, Emperor 73
Tlatlico 68
Tomaco, Bay of 108
Trepanning 21
Trimborn, Hermann 55
Troy 76, 82, 93
Trujillo 34
Tula 22–4, 27
Tunja 132, 155
    Stones 155–7, 159, 161, 168, 204
Twain, Mark 102

Universidad de los Andes 102
Urim (oracle stone) 3, 5, 6
Utah 5
Utnapishtim 16–18, 29

Veracruz 68
Viracocha (God) 162

Washington, George 158
Wedemeyer, Inge von 56
Whitmer, Christian 6
Whitmer, David 6
Whitmer, Jacob 6
Whitmer, John 6
Whitmer, Peter Jnr 6
Willey, Gordon R. 64

Yanomano Indians 202–4
Yaro (River) 108
Yucatán 25

Zantana 182
Zapotecs 68
Zedekia 27
Ziusudra 18, 29

Ancient Astronaut Society
World Headquarters
1921 St Johns Avenue
Highland Park
Illinois 60035
USA
Telephone: (312) 432-6230

Dear Reader,

Last but not least, may I introduce to you the Ancient Astronaut Society, abbreviated to AAS. It is a tax-exempt, non-profit membership society. It was founded in the USA in 1973. It now has members in more than 50 countries.

The Society's objective is the collection, exchange and publication of evidence tending to support and confirm the following theories:

The earth received a visit from outer space in prehistoric times ... (or)
The present technical civilisation on our planet is not the first ... (or)
A combination of both theories.

Membership of the AAS is open to everybody. A newsletter for members is published in English and German every two months. The AAS takes part in the organisation of expeditions and study journeys to archaeological and other sites of importance for the proof of the theory. A world congress takes place every year. Previous congresses were held in Chicago (1974), Zürich (1975), Crikvenica, Yugoslavia (1976), Rio de Janeiro (1977), Chicago (1978), Munich (1979), Auckland, New Zealand (1980), Vienna (1982).

Please write directly to the Society for membership information and a free copy of the Society's newsletter *Ancient Skies*.

Most sincerely,
Erich von Däniken